* 1,000,000 *
Free E-Books
@
www.ForgottenBooks.org

* Alchemy *
The Secret is Revealed
@
www.TheBookofAquarius.com

How Criminals Are Made and Prevented

A Retrospect of Forty Years

By

J. W. Horsley

HOW CRIMINALS ARE MADE AND PREVENTED
A RETROSPECT OF FORTY YEARS

BY

J. W. HORSLEY, M.A.,

VICAR OF DETLING, KENT; HON.
CANON OF SOUTHWARK; LATE AND
LAST CHAPLAIN OF CLERKENWELL PRISON;
AUTHOR OF "JOTTINGS FROM JAIL"
"PRISONS AND PRISONERS," "I REMEMBER"
ETC.

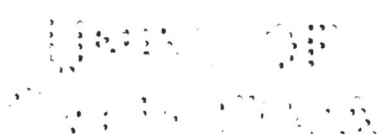

T. FISHER UNWIN
LONDON: ADELPHI TERRACE
LEIPSIC: INSELSTRASSE 20

First Published 1913

(All rights reserved.)

TO

MY SONS-IN-LAW,

PRIESTS AND PROPHETS BOTH.

280208

CONTENTS

CHAPTER I

HISTORY OF CLERKENWELL PRISON 9

From 1615 to 1886—Evil conditions before Howard's visits—Rebuilding and improvement—Becomes a House of Detention for those on remand or awaiting trial or detained in default of bail—The Fenian explosion—Its plan and structure—Chapels ancient and modern.

CHAPTER II

SOME OF MY CHARGES 34

Charles Peace—A portrait-gallery of "some of the worst."

CHAPTER III

COMMERCIAL MORALITY TENDING TO CRIME . . 38

Necessity of more teaching of morals—Prevalence of a low standard—Some causes; the influence of the "galled jade"; the depreciation of "merely moral" teaching; the neglect of definite moral teaching for the young—Innate ideal of honesty or "righteousness"—Vicious maxims of trade—*Caveat emptor*—The price of a thing is what it will fetch—Findings, keepings—All's fair in love and war and business—Honesty is the best policy—One must live—Honesty in word—Perjury common and unchecked—Half-truths—Exaggera-

Contents

PAGE

tion—Cant—Benefit of calling a spade a spade in moral matters—Commercial immorality not rare — Ubiquity of adulteration — Excessive profit — Interest becoming usury — Perquisites—Illicit commissions—False weights and measures—Lying advertisements —Employers teaching dishonesty—Responsibility of manufacturers, and of customers—Cheating companies thought venial—Each class and occupation its own temptation—Causes of commercial immorality —Haste to be made rich—Covetousness—Due to the indiscriminate respect paid to "wealth"—And the love of luxury—Are we improving?—Remedies for the evil: conferences, power of trades unions, systematic benevolence, other synchronous pursuits, the courage to be poor.

The moral code of David—Catechisms of morality in Psalm xv—in Psalm xxiv—in Psalm xxxiv—in Psalm xxxvi—Study also Isaiah xxxiii, 14 and 15, for another moral catechism with six tests of integrity as regards trickery, untruth, cheating, bribery, cruelty, and lust—The responsibility of Parliament, journalists, and novelists —Necessity of restitution—When and how to be made.

CHAPTER IV

DRINK-CAUSED CRIME 132

What proportion—Returns from South London police-courts—Extent and increase of female intemperance—Census of drinkers in Lambeth and Battersea—The barmaid question—The Judicial statistics understate the truth.

CHAPTER V

BETTING AS A CAUSE OF CRIME 159

Increase of the evil—What appeared a generation ago and what appears now—Betting and embezzlement—Football in danger—The iniquity of providing, and the absurdity of believing in, "sporting prophets."

Contents

CHAPTER VI

SAVE THE BABE 182

Excessive infantile death-rate—Its dietetic causes—Slums infanticidal—Ignorance of mothers—Decrease of birth-rate—Necessity for school clinics and feeding—Evasion of the duty—Prevalence of bad health and physique—Necessity of forewarning and forearming children against intoxicants.

CHAPTER VII

TRANSFORM THE LAD 211

Child-saving work—The transformation of human waste—Heredity omnipotent?—Or environment?—Change the environment—Educate Free Will—Apply the force of grace—Effects of elementary education neither great nor permanent unless supplemented and developed—Its elements often evanescent—The origin and natural history of the hooligan—How he may be transformed.

CHAPTER VIII

SOME USEFUL BOOKS ON CRIME 234

Literature on crime and criminals—A representative group to study: Dr. McConnell's "Criminal Responsibility" (Determinism the sole cause); Dr. Albert Wilson's "Education, Personality, and Crime" (Biology the sole remedy); Sir Robert Anderson's "Crime and Criminals" (the protection of society); "Known to the Police," Mr. Thomas Holmes (notes of a field naturalist, not a theoretical student); "Crime and Criminals" and "The Modern Prison Curriculum," both by Dr. Quinton (sane observations and suggestions of a prison doctor and governor); "The Criminal and the Community," Dr. Devon, a prison doctor in Glasgow (of unequal interest and value); "Juvenile Offenders," Rev. W. D. Morrison (illuminative on the causes and remedies of juvenile delinquency);

Contents

"Young Gaol-birds," C. E. B. Russell (sketches of typical young criminals); "Punishment and Prevention of Crime," Sir E. DuCane (prison history and reform).

CHAPTER IX

ARE WE IMPROVING? 269

Optimistic generalizations on a retrospect of thirty-nine years—External manifestations of vice—Legal aids still needed—Temperance progress—Sanitary and housing reform — Town Planning Act—Progress in prison reform—Children and the law—Improvement in schools—Home comforts more possible—More or less religion?

ILLUSTRATIONS

THE AUTHOR	*Frontispiece*	
PLAN OF THE HOUSE OF DETENTION, CLERKENWELL	*Facing p.*	29
THE RIGHT-HAND WING, HOUSE OF DETENTION, CLERKENWELL	,,	30
AN OLD-FASHIONED PRISON CHAPEL . .	,,	32
A MODERN PRISON CHURCH . . .	,,	34
CONTEMPORARIES OF CHARLES PEACE . .	,,	36
CHARLES PEACE	,,	234
LEAVENWORTH PENITENTIARY, KANSAS . .	,,	260

HOW CRIMINALS ARE MADE AND PREVENTED

CHAPTER I

HISTORY OF CLERKENWELL PRISON

"LATE and last Chaplain of H.M. Prison, Clerkenwell"—so have I seen myself described on many a bill calling attention to a meeting which I was to address on intemperance, betting, commercial immorality, the housing of the poor, milk adulteration, food reform, prison reform, workhouse and Poor Law reform, and other social subjects; and as the ten years I spent in that prison were worth twenty spent outside as regards their educational effect on the mind of one who wanted to know the causes of, and the remedies for, many of the complex social problems of his day, I may be pardoned if I begin this book with an historical sketch of that prison, especially

How Criminals are Made and Prevented

as thereby evidence will incidentally be given of the progress of prison reform.

We must go back very nearly three hundred years to find that in 1615 a large garden in Clerkenwell was bought by the Middlesex Justices for the punishment and employment (the latter being often the former) of rogues and vagabonds. Hitherto, these had been accommodated in the City Bridewell; but they were so increasing in number that the City Fathers began to discover that it was not their duty to be burdened with them. The site and the building cost only £2,500, part of which came from a county rate, part by " the free gift of the justices," and £500 given by the City was spent on building and furnishing, although it had been earmarked " to make a stock for the employment of the poor," for though it was called a House of Correction, it, apparently, was intended to have some of the characteristics of an Elizabethan workhouse. It had hardly been finished when the larky larrikins of the City 'prentices, who held a kind of Saturnalia each Shrove Tuesday, " had a cast at the New Bridewell beyond St. John Street," according to Strype, probably because some of their number had been sent thither, and possibly found the fare

History of Clerkenwell Prison

not equal to that of the City. In the State papers it is always called the New Prison, and not House of Correction or Bridewell, and it was used from the first for the incarceration of Roman Catholic priests and others, some of whom were occasionally released at the request of the Spanish or of the Venetian ambassador on the promise that they should be sent abroad, while Earl Gondomar received one John Collington, priest, into his house "on promise to give no scandal to any, he being old and infirm." Sometimes a search was made in the prison for "popish books, massing stuff, and other relics of popery." Two masters and a matron had been appointed to rule and employ the prisoners, and apparently from the first they had failed in humanity, for, in 1621, Thomas Newton complained that he had languished for four years from bruises, etc., caused by the ill-usage of Aquila Wykes, keeper, and had been thirteen weeks in a dungeon without fire or air. Passing on for forty years, Pepys and his wife go thither to see Mrs. Margaret Pen, "who is at school in Clerkenwell," an early use of such euphemisms as the more modern "His Majesty's Teetotal Hotel." Again, on a Shrove Tuesday, in 1668, the 'prentices besieged the prison and rescued therefrom some

How Criminals are Made and Prevented

of their friends who had been sent there that day for putting-down brothels, "one of the great grievances of the nation." And so Pepys records that the military had to be called out "as if the French were coming to the town."

There was, of course, no chaplain in those days; but if there had been his task would have been a perplexing one, since with the Romans were plenty of Nonconformists of the Protestant variety —a curious, unhappy family when the poet Taylor calls the place, in 1630, "a jayle for hereticks, For Brownists, Familists, and Schismaticks." Also others were committed for blasphemy, some of whom were plainly, from the utterances which were their condemnation, simply lunatics. Taylor's poem, by the by, was entitled "The Vertue of a jayle and the necessitie of hanging." Amongst these curiously commingled religionists and irreligionists the most eminent was undoubtedly Richard Baxter, who, if he had allowed or applauded the earlier conviction of Churchmen for the possession of a prayer-book, found that others besides Cromwell and the anti-Church party could be intolerant. His offence was that of preaching in his own house at Acton, contrary to the 1662 Act of Uniformity. We are glad, however, to learn

History of Clerkenwell Prison

from his testimony that the evil treatment of forty years earlier was, at any rate, not his experience. He wrote: " My imprisonment was no great suffering to me, for I had an honest jaylor, who shewed me all the kindness he could. I had a large room, and liberty to walk in a fair garden, and my wife was never so cheerful a companion to me as in prison, and was very much against my seeking to be released; and she brought me so many necessaries that we kept house as contentedly and comfortably as at home, though in a narrower; and I had a sight of more friends in a day than I had at home in half a year." First Division prisoners of our times, please note! Here he published the second part of a tract, "Directions to the Converted"; but though he had been sent for six months "without bail or mainprize" he had friends at Court, and was released by the Court of Common Pleas on the ground of an informality in the document which had sent him to prison.

Passing on nearly a hundred years, a pamphleteer confined here for an improper use of his pen, set to work, like most scribblers who find their way to prison in our days, to make "copy" out of his experiences, and no doubt with greater justification than the many vendors of "prison 'orrors"

How Criminals are Made and Prevented

who have succeeded him. His name was Jacob Ilive, and he describes graphically the unrestrained intercourse and even debauchery of the male and female inmates, and the wretched accommodation given them unless they could make a sixpenny lodging-house out of the prison, while the overcrowding of the place caused sixty or seventy women to be in two wards, each only seven and a half feet square. So he says; but arithmetic rather suggests exaggeration. But no doubt he was quite accurate in saying that the county allowance of food was only a pennyworth of bread a day, though some were helped by Quakers who sent in broth, meat, and broken victuals from their work-building adjoining the prison, which had been a workhouse but now was used by them as an almshouse and an orphanage. This pamphlet gives what is probably the earliest plan of the earliest prison on this site. It shows twelve wards and a yard in which, at exercise time, the male and female prisoners played all sorts of games, from hunt the slipper to tossing, while on Sundays the early Methodists were allowed to preach. This was in 1757. In 1764, a woman was carted from Clerkenwell Bridewell to Enfield, and publicly whipped by the common hangman for cutting down wood in Enfield

History of Clerkenwell Prison

Chase. We now come to the time of the glorious John Howard. He visited it once in 1774, twice in 1776, and once in 1777. It may be interesting here to give a list of the London prisons then in use, with the number of their inmates in 1776.

Prison.	Debtors.	Criminals.	Total.
Newgate	51	141	292
Fleet	184	—	184
Bridewell	—	13	13
Borough Compter	16	2	18
Clerkenwell	—	45	45
Clerkenwell Bridewell	—	171	171
King's Bench	498	—	498
Marshalsea	92	—	92
New Ludgate	15	—	15
Poultry Compter	46	—	46
Savoy	—	98	98
Tothill Fields Bridewell	—	74	74
Whitechapel	5	—	5
Wood Street Compter	38	11	49
Tower Hamlets	—	1	1
The Tower	—	—	0
St. Catherine's	—	—	0
Westminster Gate House	—	—	0
Totals	945	556	1501

Exactly a hundred years after this, when I entered Clerkenwell Prison, none of these buildings existed, except the disused Tower and part of Newgate. Howard found that the keeper, Edward Hall, had no salary, which meant that he made what he could

How Criminals are Made and Prevented

out of the necessities of the prisoners (a state of affairs found in some of the American prisons to this day!) and by keeping a public-house for the sale of beer and wine in the prison. The chaplain of the new New Prison, lately erected next door, came in on Thursdays only, the number of prisoners varying from 87 in 1774 to 136 in 1776, and had his salary of £50 from the New Prison, where he officiated twice on Sundays and twice in the week, although the number of prisoners was not half that of the Bridewell. There was also a surgeon, Mr. Gibbes, for the two prisons, at a salary of £60. The allowance for prisoners was a penny loaf daily. Improvement, however, had arrived since the days of Ilive, twenty years before, for the men and women had separate wards and exercise yards ; but still for beds 3s. 6d. a week had to be paid. Of the ordinary wards "one was so crowded that some prisoners slept in hammocks hung to the ceiling." The building was out of repair, and had not been white-washed for years. " I saw but few at work ; sometimes none at all." The women were apparently sleeping three in each of some " dark unwholesome night-rooms, 9 feet by 7 feet each : " in some of them beds for those who pay." Over thirty prisoners had long terms, up to six years;

History of Clerkenwell Prison

"they complained to me of sore feet, which the Turnkey said were quite black." In 1779, it contained 171 prisoners, of whom 22 men and boys and 58 women were convicts. Their allowance was a pound loaf and twopence a day. They picked oakum and beat hemp, the profits of which employment gave them shoes and stockings.

In 1780, the year of the great "No Popery" riots, the prison was attacked, and the keeper at once threw open the gates and released the prisoners, whereupon the mob retired.

A new prison having been built adjoining in 1775, and another in Cold Bath Fields in 1794, as a House of Correction for the county, this old Clerkenwell Bridewell was pulled down in or about 1804.

The New Prison, Clerkenwell, called when rebuilt in 1818 the Middlesex House of Detention, was pulled down and rebuilt on larger and more modern lines in 1845, on tne plan of what was then called the Model Prison at Pentonville, the name remaining until it became H.M. Prison, Clerkenwell, in 1877. This New Prison was a "chapel of ease" to overcrowded Newgate. One of its early prisoners was Jack Sheppard with his paramour Edgeworth Bess. Visiting friends having

How Criminals are Made and Prevented

brought in a file, fetters were broken, window-bars removed, and blanket ropes let them down twenty-five feet into a yard. The difficulty presented by the outer wall and its *chevaux de frise* was overcome by their utilizing the bolts, bars, and locks of the entrance gate as steps.

John Howard found, in 1776, a gaoler, James Elmore, with the large salary of £30 with, of course, the profits of the prison tap. All the inmates were felons, and varied on his several visits from 37 to 87. The building was a great improvement on the older buildings; well ventilated was each room, "but, very properly, no glass." There was also the modern innovation of a chapel, which was to be available also for the Bridewell next door. "No infirmary: no bedding or straw." A matron had £5 out of the gaoler's £30. For the privilege of entering the prison each felon paid 1s. 4d. for garnish or footing. "Pay or strip" was the rule, and if the new convict had no money part of his or her scanty apparel (which had to serve also for bedding) had to be given up. Yet Mark Tapley's ancestor seems to have been among them, for the *Public Advertiser* of September 8, 1775, says: "The prisoners removed yesterday to Newgate behaved with the utmost impudence. Two sets of

History of Clerkenwell Prison

them linked in chains, one from the New Prison and the other from Bridewell, ran a race which should get first to Newgate, which was won by the latter." In 1780, the mob that secured the opening and the clearing of the Bridewell encountered some opposition here, and had to break open the door and gates with pickaxes, and so released the prisoners. Next year there was a prison riot, headed by one to whom a visitor had brought in a sword (queer searching in those days!) and eventually three prisoners were killed and twelve wounded by soldiers firing "into the brown" in the exercise yard.

Then, in 1818, the New Prison was enlarged and practically rebuilt, the site of the old Clerkenwell Bridewell being taken in, and a boundary wall was erected at a cost of nearly £5,000. This wall remained unto my time, and part of it still remains and shows the effects of the gap blown in it by the Fenians in 1867. The rebuilding took two years, and cost upwards of £35,000, with accommodation for 240 prisoners, each in a separate cell.

After a lapse of twenty-seven years, however, another rebuilding took place, and a larger prison was erected in 1846, on the model of Pentonville. It was now to be a House of Detention for uncon-

How Criminals are Made and Prevented

victed persons on remand, or those in default of bail, and deserters, the House of Correction at Cold Bath Fields (also in Clerkenwell) receiving convicted prisoners. The accommodation was for 324 prisoners in separate cells, and gas was installed. Later on, another wing was added to increase accommodation, and when this was not needed for those on remand or awaiting trial, it was used as an overflow place for Cold Bath Fields. Here, and now, of course, began daily services, and the appointment of a chaplain in the modern fashion. Hepworth Dixon, who wrote on "The London Prisons" in 1850, says the one great fault was the size of the prison (this was before the new wing was built), the building coming too near the wall, and making the prison therefore neither very airy nor very safe. At that time the detained persons had permission to work for themselves or for any one who would employ them. What chiefly struck him was apparently the utter slumminess of the whole neighbourhood as approached from Holborn. Fear was then just beginning to cry out for sanitation. "Respectability has become alarmed for its own safety. . . . By means of such agents as fever and cholera, the mass of putrefying humanity has asserted its

History of Clerkenwell Prison

intimate connexion with all other sorts of humanity." When the truth was felt that white kid and Russian sables were no protection against the contagion of misery-made diseases, then philanthropy began to flourish in high places. Of Field Lane he remarks: " The dwellings on either side are dark; in some of them candles or gas is burning all day long. The stench is awful. Along the middle of the narrow lane runs a gutter into which every sort of poisonous liquid is poured. This thoroughfare is occupied entirely by receivers of stolen goods, which goods are openly spread out for sale. . . . No wonder to find a gaol in such a neighbourhood! The flavour of the fruit depends upon the quality of the soil: and here we have some of the richest rankness in the world." The *détenues* came only from Middlesex, and so I found it in 1876; but soon after my appointment Horsemonger Lane was abolished, in 1878, and we received the Surrey men and women, the latter, coming mainly from Southwark and riparian South London, being declared by the female warders to be much lower in type and behaviour than those from Middlesex. Horsemonger Lane, the site of which is now a playground in my old borough of Southwark, was one of the 37 prisons closed when Government

How Criminals are Made and Prevented

took over the prisons from the county authorities. There were thus 113 prisons in England and Wales in 1877, and 69 in 1878. There are now 56 local prisons and 3 convict prisons.

In Mayhew's "Criminal Prisons of London," published in 1860, everything seems to be as I found it in 1876, but the statistics he gives for that year are worth notice. There had entered in the year for trial 1,170 males, 439 females. In default of bail, 577 males, 168 females. Remanded and discharged, 3,595 males, 1,534 females. Deserters, 303 males. Total commitments, 5,645 males and 2,141 females. An improvement which came about twenty years later was plainly needed when we find that there were 185 boys and 27 girls under twelve years of age, and in addition 736 boys and 156 girls under sixteen. Even at the beginning of my time I had children of six and seven years remanded! There were 1,281 males and 697 females who on reception were unable to read or write, a number now, of course, tremendously reduced, although, as I show later in this book, education has not yet done all it is supposed to do. The number of absolute illiterates recorded is always somewhat under the truth when based on statements made at reception, since some are

History of Clerkenwell Prison

ashamed to admit the fact, and others know that if they profess some power to read they will get library books in which there are pictures to look at. That sanitation and diet had vastly improved is shown by the facts that in the year there had been but one death (though the bail prisoners, who numbered 745, were here for a considerable time, even up to twelve months), never more than 9 sick at one time, and only 176 infirmary cases in the year.

The only especially memorable events in the subsequent history of the prison were the Fenian Explosion in 1867, its being taken over by the Government, its closing, and its transformation into a school.

What happened was this. Two Fenians, Burke and Casey, who were afterwards hanged, were awaiting trial in the House of Detention, and on Thursday, December 12th, Sir Richard Mayne, the Commissioner of Police, in consequence of information received from Dublin, sent a warning to Captain Codd that the wall near the exercise ground would be undermined in order to rescue the Fenian prisoners. The Governor had suggested, when Groves, another Fenian, was in the prison, that a cordon of police should keep

How Criminals are Made and Prevented

people away from the walls, as he "would take care of the kernel if the police took care of the shell," but unfortunately this was not done then or on this occasion. Therefore, in the afternoon of Friday, two men, Allen and Desmond, and a woman named Ann Justice, took into Corporation Row, which runs parallel to the north wall of the prison and consisted of small houses crowded with poor people, a barrel on a truck, into which, after borrowing a light from a boy who was smoking, Desmond thrust a squib, and at a quarter to four (when presumably the prisoners would be exercising in the yard) the explosion occurred, and was heard for miles round. It blew down houses and shattered the windows of others in all directions, and most of the prison windows, and made a breach in the wall sixty feet across. Upwards of forty people, men, women, and children of all ages, some of whom happened to be passing, while most were in their houses, were injured more or less severely, and four were killed or died in hospital. After the smoke had cleared away a crowd of people rushed through the breach in the wall. Captain Codd, not knowing what the object of some might be, bade them disperse. They hesitated, upon which he ordered a volley

History of Clerkenwell Prison

with blank cartridge to be fired and the gapers took to their heels panic-stricken, and the ground was cleared of the intruders in less than five minutes. A box made by the prison engineer out of the staves and the hoops of the barrel is in the possession of the Codd family. Five hundred police were then put on duty to keep off the crowd and preserve order, and a hundred of the Fusilier Guards were on guard in the prison during the night. Amongst the victims in St. Bartholomew's Hospital were children aged 13, 11, 8, 8, 5, 4, "two other boys" and a child not known, and a baby (unclaimed). In the Free Hospital were three other children aged four, and a boy of two and a half. The three culprits were speedily traced and apprehended, and the woman tried to strangle herself in the prison, but the attempt was frustrated. A large sum was given by the public in aid of the families who had suffered. The Duke of Connaught, as Prince Arthur, attended by Dr. Jenner, visited all the sufferers in the Free Hospital, and among the visitors to the prison were the Prince of Wales and the Duke of Cambridge. William and Timothy Desmond, Nicholas English, John O'Keefe, Michael Barrett, and Ann Justice were

How Criminals are Made and Prevented

tried at the Central Criminal Court for complicity in the explosion on April 20, 1868. Justice was acquitted on April 23rd, O'Keefe on April 24th, the two Desmonds and English on April 27th. Barrett alone was convicted on April 27th, and was hanged in Newgate on May 26th.

Several things contributed to the passing of the Prisons Act in 1877. In spite of the Prisons Act of 1865, which was to abolish discrepancies of treatment in the county prisons, uniformity in punishment had not been secured, buildings in some places were bad, and unnecessary expense was caused by the multitude of prisons, and especially by the small size of many of them. And that two thousand justices could not adequately supervise or know the prisons they only periodically visited had been made evident by the revelations made during the investigation into Birmingham Borough Gaol in 1850, which forms the foundation of Charles Reade's novel and play, "Never too Late to Mend." Also Government wanted to relieve local taxes. Henceforth, a body of Prison Commissioners, under the Home Secretary, had entire responsibility, and uniformity, efficiency, and economy ensued. Clerkenwell was especially interested in the new rules put out, as some of

History of Clerkenwell Prison

them provided for the much better treatment of the unconvicted prisoners, and also of those detained in default of bail, for which two classes the prison continued chiefly to exist. Now, discipline, diet, and clothing were uniform, and the mark system encouraged good behaviour, so that the daily average number of punishments per 1,000 prisoners, which was 8·5 in 1877, came down to 5·8 in 1882. Hitherto, a more liberal dietary recommended by the Home Office in 1843 was only adopted by 63 out of 140 local prisons, and another framed in 1864 was taken only by 26 out of 116. Now, however, the era of one diet, a better diet, and a less costly diet, set in. Also the number of superior officers was reduced (by the closing of small prisons) from 446 to 233, at a saving of nearly £41,000 per annum. And lastly, a general decrease in crime, or rather in commitments to prison, caused in 1886 a closing of Clerkenwell Prison, preceded by the closing of Horsemonger Lane, of Westminster, of Cold Bath Fields, while Newgate ceased in 1882 to be used as an ordinary prison and was attached for administrative purposes to Clerkenwell while it existed, and then to Holloway, being used only for the lodging of those awaiting trial at the

How Criminals are Made and Prevented

sittings of the Central Criminal Court. On April 20, 1886, therefore, I bade farewell to the scene of my labours for ten years, during which I had about 100,000 under my care of both sexes, all ages, unconvicted and convicted, coming from an area of which the extreme points were Enfield and Croydon, Stratford and Staines. Of all conditions and ranks were they, from the street-arab urchin to those who had known high life. One month we had either detained or on the calendar awaiting trial but out on bail, a prince, a baron, a marchioness, and two lords. All the murderers of Middlesex and Surrey came to us, all the deserters in the Metropolitan area, dynamiters and police officials, three hundred or so each year who had attempted self-murder and were sent for my exhortation to them and my report to the magistrates, juveniles and women sent that I might find Homes for them or other ways of helping those who desired and were worthy of aid rather than punishment, cranks and dipsomaniacs, beggars and company-promoters, so that the knowledge of human nature in all its phases and varieties gained was such, that I used to desire that every young clergyman should have some time as a prison chaplain as part of his training.

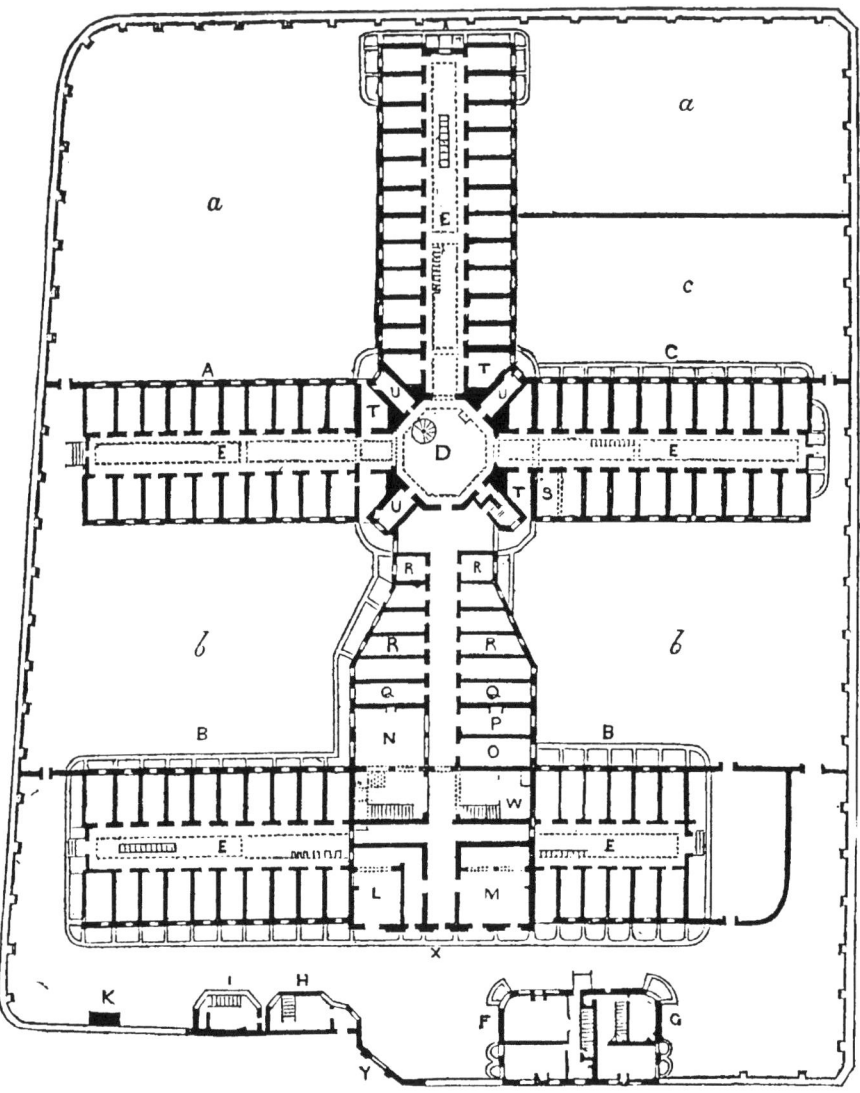

PLAN OF THE HOUSE OF DETENTION, CLERKENWELL.

A and C. Male wings. B. Female wing. D. Central hall. E. Passages. F. Governor's house. G. Garden (afterwards Matron's house). H and I. Porter's Lodge. K. Office (afterwards Chief Warder's house). L. Entry to Female Ward. M. Clerks' office. N. Warders' mess-room. O and P. Waiting-rooms. Q. Solicitors' rooms R. Reception cells. S. and T. Refractory cells. W. Governor's office. X. Entry to main building. Y. Large prison gate. *a, b, c.* Exercising yards.

History of Clerkenwell Prison

The illustration opposite represents the House of Detention as I knew it, except that the bird's-eye view does not show the more recently erected wing which ran at right angles to the second block on the right-hand side, and there should be the porter's lodgings and the chief warder's house to the left of the entrance. My office was made of two cells knocked into one, and from it I could look out to the right of the prisoners represented as exercising. From its aspect the sun never entered the windows during the time I was at work, a fact which mattered little to me but much to the prisoners whose cells looked out to the same point of the compass. A warder would hardly be discoursing with a lady visitor at the big gates, which were only opened for the prison van or coal carts. The small entrance for officers and visitors and prisoners arriving on foot was to the left. The prison van, or " Black Maria," bore the royal initials on its side, and I remember once having to pacify a lunatic who had to be removed to an asylum. He did not want to go anywhere. " Oh, but the Queen has sent a carriage for you." " A carriage? What, one of them with V.R. on the side?" " Yes, that stands for her name, Victoria Regina, you know." " No,

How Criminals are Made and Prevented

it don't: it stands for Vagabonds Removed." Insanity had not bereft him of reason. The illustration opposite represents the right-hand wing taken from the central and octagonal hall. The ground floor cells to the right were "special" cells, *i.e.*, those in which murderers were confined and others who might be inclined to attempt suicide. Lights were so arranged that they could be inspected at any moment, and warders had to look in at short intervals night and day. The lift for trays of rations has come up from the kitchen in the basement, and is seen on the third floor. The doors in the angle to the left were of cells used as infirmaries; not that they were often needed. In the uppermost one I can well remember visiting, until he died, an old actor named Harcourt, who was in for defacing coinage in a way difficult to detect but not very profitable. I must not, of course, describe the process. My office would be at the end of the upper gallery on the left, and many, many times a day did I have to run up and down the circular or the sloping iron stairs. The upper gallery seems rather dizzy, and thereby hangs a tale. In Parliament lately it was suggested that a certain suffragette, as a protest or in despair, leaped over the gallery as

THE RIGHT-HAND WING, HOUSE OF DETENTION, CLERKENWELL.

History of Clerkenwell Prison

if to commit suicide. The incident is particularly interesting to me because a young soldier one day acted in this manner, broke his neck, and died on the spot. Shortly after that I was standing in the octagon talking to the chief warder, while the prisoners were going in to the daily service. A man suddenly appeared by our side on the ground floor. The chief warder said, "You have come the wrong way, my man. Up those steps again." This prisoner, it was afterwards found, had jumped over the gallery and alighted on his feet unhurt; but going up again he leaped a second time and killed himself. I had to go out to break the news to his family. In consequence, I wrote to the Prison Commissioners, and experiments were made. We had wire netting stretched between the pathways of the first gallery, and then filled sacks to the weight of the average man and threw them from the top gallery, and found they would not break through. Then the warders walked on the netting, and no hole resulted. Since then the system has been adopted wherever needed, so that if any one were to leap they would simply bounce up on the resilient netting. If the suffragette intended to commit suicide she was ignorant of the fact that she could not do it that

How Criminals are Made and Prevented

way. A daily paper, commenting on my narration of this incident in a lecture, said, "How dare the Canon deny the suffragette the right to break her neck? This is another exhibition of the villainy of man!"

I have no picture of our chapel, in which I officiated in a gallery with the women on an opposite gallery invisible to the men who were on rising rows of seats beneath me; but the illustration opposite will give some idea of how religious impressions and reformation were aided by the beauty of holiness. As a contrast, see opposite p. 34, the interior of the chapel of a modern prison.

The separate boxes were supposed to render communication impossible, but were not efficacious in this respect. Our organ, by the by, was a barrel organ which played six hymn tunes and two chants! I speedily disused it and trusted to the *vox humana* for our daily hymns.

It will be observed in the ground plan of the House of Detention that its rationale is an adaptation of Jeremy Bentham's plan of prison arrangement called by him a "panopticon," the idea being that of wings radiating from a central point

AN OLD-FASHIONED PRISON CHAPEL.

History of Clerkenwell Prison

which should command a view of all the galleries and the doors of all cells. Pentonville Prison was erected later on the same plan, after the fashion of a star-fish with its five rays. It never occurred to people that in such a building some parts would never see or feel the sun. Contrast with this the very recently erected Leavenworth Penitentiary in Kansas standing on thirteen acres in an open country and providing for twelve hundred prisoners. (See illustration facing page 260.)

CHAPTER II

SOME OF MY CHARGES

CHARLES PEACE, the astute and inventive burglar, who was hanged eventually for murder, was under my care for some weeks on remand. In appearance he resembled a half-caste crossing-sweeper more than the bold burglar, and he was a proper old humbug until his guilt could no longer be denied. But he put a truth effectively before me when he said in my first talk with him, "If a minister really believed in his work it would pay him not merely to go a Sabbath day's journey to preach, but to go there on his hands and knees on broken bottles." I have heard the same thought not so adhesively put by bishops and conductors of spiritual retreats.

Owing to the unnecessary prominence given to every detail of his career by fevered pressmen in search of copy, many had their thoughts turned to burglary as a substitute for work, and to imitate him by carrying a revolver became a fashion

A MODERN PRISON CHURCH.

From a photograph supplied by the Church Army.

Some of My Charges

amongst thieves, whereby several murders came about. The mere possession of such a weapon, useful only for homicide, should be in England made an offence, and an armed criminal should always have an additional sentence. I drew attention to the fashion, its origin, and its increase, many years ago in the *Echo*, but hoped then that the fashion would pass. On the contrary, it has so increased by tolerance that now we think we are obliged to give revolvers to our police.

Some of Peace's contemporaries are represented in the appended group of photographs, as to which people may exercise their fancy as to whether dangerous criminals have a type of face which would warn the innocent or the unsuspecting.

1. A dangerous thief, using his trade as a house-painter to discover opportunities. Had penal servitude, and became a receiver of stolen property.
2. A sailor and river thief. Had two years, seven years, eight years, and four previous smaller sentences, though only thirty-nine.
3. A dangerous ticket-of-leave man from Yorkshire.
4. An old Southwark professional thief, though posing as a hawker. Has had two terms of penal servitude and six previous convictions.
5. Another dangerous ticket-of-leave man from Yorkshire.
6. Russian by birth, a dangerous ticket-of-leave man from Yorkshire, well tattooed.

How Criminals are Made and Prevented

7. A clever Cockney burglar, had five years' penal servitude, but escaped identification lately, when in burglary he pl nned his two companions got ten years each. One of his *aliases* was Sage and another Sausage.

8. Another Yorkshire ticket-of-leave man, well tattooed. Seven convictions including penal servitude. A dangerous character.

9. Engineer, born in India, wanted in Yorkshire, a ticket-of-leave man with six convictions, although only twenty-eight.

10. Well-educated hotel and jewel thief. Seven *aliases*. An annual conviction. Cork leg.

11. Housebreaker, ticket-of-leave man, wanted at Hull, a dangerous character.

12. Not a criminal, save as wanted for embezzling rates in Yorkshire.

13. Not a criminal, save as wanted for stealing wines and spirits as a licensed victualler at Liverpool.

14. Well-dressed railway and race-course thief. Has had seven years' penal servitude.

15. Sailor from Hartlepool, a dangerous man, on ticket.

16. Long-firm swindler. Corn-dealer from Herts. Has had five years' penal servitude.

17. Dangerous thief on ticket. Yorkshire.

18. Solicitor, wanted for embezzlement in South Shields.

19. Dangerous character from Cardiff. Had seven years for robbery with violence. Well tattooed.

20. Notorious horse-stealer of Hull. Six convictions running up to eighteen months, and seven years' supervision.

21. Dangerous Yorkshire burglar on ticket from five years' penal servitude.

22. "The Little Captain." Various convictions for uttering counterfeit coin in London. Last conviction, five years.

23. Dangerous Yorkshire housebreaker on ticket from seven years.

CONTEMPORARIES OF CHARLES PEACE.

Some of My Charges

24. Dangerous Yorkshire female thief. Ten convictions including eight years' penal, although only twenty-eight.

25. Had seven years' and ten years' penal servitude. Last conviction for a large silk larceny in London.

26. On ticket from ten years' penal. Yorkshire man.

27. Yorkshire groom. Dangerous character. On ticket from ten years' penal. Had seven years and four years' penal before, and other convictions.

28. Notorious Lancashire burglar and churchbreaker Well tattooed. Had two terms of penal servitude.

29. Notts stockbroker, wanted as absconding bankrupt and for false pretences.

30. Cockney-Irish travelling thief. Has had seven years' penal servitude.

31. London labourer, pickpocket and receiver, on ticket.

32. Croydon engineer. Thief, on ticket.

33. Dangerous London thief. Has had seven years' penal servitude.

CHAPTER III

COMMERCIAL MORALITY TENDING TO CRIME

IN none of the books on crime and its causes which I possess is there any mention of a low standard of commercial morality as a great cause of offences against property, and indeed religion as a preventive of evil is commonly spoken of as something apart from morality, and when marvels are hoped from the spread of education it is the intellectual rather than the moral element therein which is generally considered. It seems, therefore, well that more attention should be drawn to the necessity of more direct moral teaching in the school and in church, and that any low standard of commercial morality which produces "tricks of trade," and trade maxims indefensible from a right moral standpoint, should be combated. Let me attempt the task.

The life of virtue is as a pyramid of three tiers, the base being formed of the four Cardinal or

Commercial Morality Tending to Crime

basal virtues of Prudence, Justice, Temperance, and Fortitude, the higher tier being Faith and Hope, while the apex is found in "the greatest of these" Theological virtues—namely, Charity or Love. Faith does not constitute the whole of the pyramid, nor will the contemplation or teaching of morality exclude the claims and the practice of the higher life to which Faith and its sister virtues lead. Yet many in all schools of thought, and most in one particular school, have looked askance at the teaching—and still more at the preaching—of what they describe as mere morality, and thereby often speak in a tongue unknown to the multitudes, and affecting them not for good. Immorality is rife, whether commercial, sexual, or political; and is largely caused by the silence or timidity or indefiniteness of those who, as parents or teachers or preachers or writers, have great opportunities, and therefore great responsibility, in this subject towards the young and the ignorant. Multitudes sin and commit crime from ignorance as much as from choice, and this ignorance arises often from their not having had a fair chance of knowledge. Their faults of commission are obvious, and universally condemned: the faults of omission on the part of those who might have

How Criminals are Made and Prevented

taught and trained them are not so commonly noticed or admitted. " These poor sheep, what have they done?" rose constantly from my heart when, as a prison chaplain, I spoke to my daily congregation or passed from cell to cell. John Bradford, the pious Puritan, saw a condemned criminal on his way from my old prison, which was then called the New Prison of Clerkenwell, to the gibbet at Tyburn, and uttered words often quoted with admiration: " There, but for the grace of God, goes John Bradford." True words, a useful thought; but better, surely, would have been the addition of the words, "and there is one for whose state John Bradford is partly responsible." More humanity, and therefore more divinity, I find in the declaration of Robertson of Brighton, " I cannot see or hear of evil without thinking that somehow I have had a finger in its creation." Meditate upon the ethical, scientific, and Scriptural truth, " No man liveth to himself"; think how the lives that seem apart, or even to be in a different zone of life, will be found interwoven on that day when the secrets and the influences of all hearts shall be revealed, and the mists which hide us one from another shall clear away, and the tangles of life straighten out; recall

Commercial Morality Tending to Crime

how what are called the "chance" words of one whom Christianity forbids us to call a stranger, have influenced our own minds or spirits for good or evil; remember how sins of omission are the chief subject of inquiry in the glimpses our Lord gave us of the principles of the General Judgment; and then something better than infertile remorse will spring from the ashes of the might-have-beens, and we shall be less ready to condemn others for immorality and more ready to condemn ourselves. The mission of Dives to his brethren would probably have been futile, stung to death by the taunt, "Why were you silent before?" or, rather, "How can we forget, or you undo, the effects and the eloquence of your daily example?"

The prevalence of bad or lax morals, of a low standard of morality, is admitted and bemoaned not least loudly by those who have partly caused it by the rarity or vagueness of their moral teaching. The sole arguments which touch myriads in a nominally Christian land are these: (1) The *argumentum ad hominem*—How would you like it yourself? (2) The question, Does it pay and will it pay in the long run? (3) The law of the land will touch you. Is it conceivable that no

How Criminals are Made and Prevented

higher arguments would obtain and prevail if moral teaching had been more common?

Let me now indicate three of the more prevalent causes of silence, or bated breath, or inoperative vagueness of speech on the part of those who, in the pulpit, or in the press, or in schools, have the opportunity and duty to be prophets, or forth-tellers of the truth as inspired and revealed by Him who came to destroy the works of the devil.

First, there is the unacknowledged, yet really felt, influence of the "galled jade." Many resent definite teaching on points of morals because it convinces them of sin and destroys their false peace and noxious comfort of mind. The prophets prophesy timorously, if at all, because the people love to have it so. "Doan illude to chicken stealin', brudder," said a negro deacon to a negro pastor, "dat am a subjec' what always frows a gloom ober dis congregation." Ask the clergy and ministers of Burton-on-Trent, of Newmarket, and of Manchester, if they find it easy to deliver their souls fully on the subjects of the evil, the causes, and the factors of intemperance, of betting, and of commercial immorality. Ask the editors of London daily papers whether they will surrender

Commercial Morality Tending to Crime

their claim to be the modern prophets of morality, or cease to report in unnecessary detail the proceedings in the Divorce Court, to establish and endow sporting prophets as part of their staff, and to issue contents bills that are intended to increase the circulation of their papers by appealing to what is prurient or morbid in the mob. A young Nonconformist preached clearly and bravely on a question of morality. "Young man," said his deacons in the vestry, "you stick to doctrine, doctrine hurts nobody." To me, after a sermon on honesty in daily life, in a West End church, it was objected by some one, who, I fear, must have been a "galled jade," "Religion was never intended to go into particulars!" And so platitudes pay, or at least are found not to empty pews or to diminish offertories, and people who either fail in the power or the desire to be particular are apt to apply very general principles to themselves.

The second reason for the dearth of moral teaching is the influence, greatest in the first part of the nineteenth century, of that school of theology in the Church which is chiefly content with the repetition of one aspect of one doctrine, one way of looking at the Redemption being preached as the one thing needful, so that the

How Criminals are Made and Prevented

larger doctrines of the Incarnation, the Resurrection, and the Ascension, the abiding High Priesthood and the results on earth of Pentecost, are practically left out of sight. To such preachers, what could in any way be called secular was treated as in no way spiritual, and to give moral instruction was held to prove an ignorance of what they called "saving truth." One result was that their hearers became largely what in their own shibboleth was called gospel-hardened, and just among them were found those who little practised the morality they had little been taught. Not because it is Celtic, but because it has been largely influenced by Calvinism, has the morality of Wales in the matters of truth, honesty, and chastity been notoriously less than it should be. It is there a matter of teaching, not of race.

The third reason, and the one I would ask members of the Church of England especially to consider, is the sad fact that so little moral teaching is given just where and when the opportunities are greatest. In Sunday Schools and in Children's Services how invaluable a basis is afforded by the Duty to our Neighbour from the Catechism if fully expanded, expounded and illustrated. In the precious half-hour of religious instruction which

Commercial Morality Tending to Crime

begins the day in most elementary schools, an opportunity is afforded which should not be lost, especially when in church schools the clergy can give or guide the teaching. And still more in the preparation for Confirmation, especially when that rite precedes, as it should, the leaving home and school for the new dangers and temptations of business or service, what a chance occurs for practical and definite instruction as to the common ways in which a low standard of morality will be presented to them in the business and the pleasure of a more independent life. The nation is crying out for moral teaching, and because the clergy are thought, with more or less justice, to give little or none, they are bidden to stand aside in favour of leader writers. There was, and in some measure still is, a terrible truth in George Eliot's early indictment of religious teachers as prophets simply of " other worldliness," who did little to help men, and especially the young, to use rightly the world which is the scene of their probation and their apprenticeship. Aubrey Moore well said in his "The Christian Doctrine of God," "Lutheranism starts with the belief that God is love : Calvinism with the conception of God as power. With the former, the desire at all costs to guard the belief

How Criminals are Made and Prevented

in the freedom of God's grace led to a morbid fear of righteousness, as if it were somehow a rival to faith. With the latter, a one-sided view of the power of God gradually obscured the fact that righteousness and justice eternally condition its exercise." Those of us who are in neither of these camps can, and must, learn, expound, and practise the laws of righteousness and morality as the help-meet and not the rival, still less the antagonist, of faith; and, while holding as definitely as any the doctrines of faith and of grace, we shall be the better able to justify God to man by upholding the science and the life of morality as the complement and the effect of a belief in God. It is because in the name of religion some have dissociated morals from religion, that men desiring morality have cried, "Let us have morals unencumbered with religion." It is for us to say, "Those which God hath joined together let no man put asunder."

Pass we from principles to details, and see how to combat the prevalent forms and adages of dishonesty which incline the young to crime.

"An honest man's the noblest work of God," said Pope. More usefully the truth might be put, " Man is God's noblest work (of which we have

Commercial Morality Tending to Crime

full knowledge), but no one is a man unless upright and righteous." St. Paul's precept, "Quit you like men," is neither directed to one sex alone, nor can it be obeyed by anything short of the harmonious development of all the powers of man, the fulfilment of all his duties, and the right life of each part of his triune nature. Happily for us, we have innate ideas of honesty: they form part of the universal or natural religion whereby "God has not left Himself without a witness in the hearts of men," whether they be within or without the pale of Christianity. Society, whether civilized or not, is only possible by the mutual faith which expects to find honesty more common than dishonesty. Thou shalt not steal, thou shalt not bear false witness, are laws that existed before they were placed in the Decalogue, and are recognized as laws by those who have never read them in the Bible. The chief difference between the heathen and the Christian ideals of honesty is that in the former glory is given to the honest, and but little shame to the dishonest; whereas in the latter shame is given to the dishonest, but no special glory to the honest, who should not expect or receive praise for being what he must be. So in the parable of the unjust steward, his lord (not

How Criminals are Made and Prevented

the Lord) has almost admiration for the cunning and foresight of the embezzling and swindling servant, even while he punishes him. Thus would the incident strike the average Eastern mind, before and outside the atmosphere of Christian feeling and practice. I know a window put up in a Town Hall as a record of the honesty of a tradesman who failed and compounded with his creditors, but some years afterwards paid them in full, though not legally obliged to do so. The moral of the window seems to me somewhat immoral, as expressing some astonishment that a man should do, from his personal conception of honesty, what neither human law nor the ordinary standard of commercial morality would compel or even suggest. Again, a man early in the nineteenth century bought two lottery tickets, one for himself and another for a friend. One day he wrote, "I congratulate you: your ticket has won a £20,000 prize." "But how did you know which was mine?" "I marked it, and put both by and forgot about them until the result of the lottery was declared." How easy to have changed the tickets, or to have held his tongue! Knaves would think him a fool for his pains, and, by their astonishment, would display their own dishonesty. Rise above the ordinary

Commercial Morality Tending to Crime

level of honesty, as we observe it amongst buyers and sellers; better still, strive in every way and on every opportunity to raise it. Do neither, and you will inevitably be dragged down to it, and then with it to even lower depths. By popular proverbs current in trade we can discover what that level is. It was said, "Let me make the songs of a nation, and I care not who makes its laws." But songs are too long to learn and to quote. Pregnant and pithy proverbs are more powerful for good and evil, and we are largely ruled by phrases. Let us consider some of these which foster dishonesty or maintain a low level of integrity and brotherly faith and action.

1. *The legal maxim,* "*Caveat emptor*"—Let the buyer look after his own interest or suffer in consequence. Fine your brother for his ignorance. Get a fair price from a sharp, and an unfair one from a flat. It is this maxim in the minds of those who traded with simple nations that has dishonoured our Christianity, and caused commercial depression at home when we have been at last found out abroad. The Dutch traders with Red Indians weighed their foot against furs while the sellers, ignorant of how scales worked, did not know that the greater part of the weight of the body could

How Criminals are Made and Prevented

be added to the foot. Never mind, we profit thereby, and *caveat emptor*. Our Lancashire cotton goods sent to the East were often loaded with 100 per cent. of China clay, and sold well. When the adulteration was found out in India and China, the sale decreased and Lancashire whined. "Calico," says a trade circular before me, "which loses half its weight in washing is palmed off on the public. It is very difficult to tell a heavily-sized from a pure calico before washing it." Sell it, however, say some, *caveat emptor*, and before we are found out we shall have made our pile, and our successors to whom we have sold the good business will suffer, not us. A year or two ago I tested the Upper Standards of St. Peter's, Walworth, School on this point. They had to answer on paper my question: "If a boy sold a pair of roller skates that were broken, and he knew it, but the purchaser did not, what would you say about it?" Only one, I was glad to find, took *caveat emptor* as his guide, but most, both boys and girls, expressed entire reprobation in unqualified terms, *e.g.*, He was a cheat—a fraud—a hypocrite—he did a very caddish trick, and I think he ought to have a good hiding. One only hopes their principles will not be broken down by prevalent custom or even the direct bidding

Commercial Morality Tending to Crime

of employers, if any find themselves behind the counter in shops, in some of which the rule is, "Cheat my customers and you shall have a bonus: cheat me, and you will be prosecuted."

2. *The price of a thing is what it will fetch.*—Partly a truism and partly a devil's proverb. Shall we finish it by adding "quite independent of the necessity or the ignorance of my brother"? Where is your worth if you consider not what the article is worth, but only what you can get for it on terms so favourable to your pocket, that they must be unfavourable to those of your brother? Ruskin, the son of a merchant, reckons the merchant among the honourable professions which have relation to our daily necessities. The soldier, the priest, the doctor, the lawyer, the merchant, all have to help the nation, and, on due occasion, to die for it. Die, rather than leave your post in battle or in pestilence. Die, rather than teach falsehood or countenance injustice. Die, merchant, rather than not produce in the purest and cheapest forms. Why is the merchant or tradesman, asks Ruskin, not held in such popular honour as the rest? Because they are not, and he is, presumed to act from selfish motives. Because, in other words, What can I get? and not What do you want? is their habitual thought.

How Criminals are Made and Prevented

The stern arm of military authority had to come down on a dealer in food during the siege of Ladysmith, who was only acting on this commercial adage and put up prices till he was put down himself.

3. *Findings, keepings.*—As honesty is a matter for the buyer as well as the seller to consider and cultivate, so also it is for the child as well as the adult, and the first bent towards commercial immorality or anti-social acquisitiveness has often been given by this school or even nursery adage. Ask a class of children if they have heard it : see if they believe it to be a law, and if they know not how to confute and despise it, give them that elementary instruction. It seems a minor matter compared with the temptations and the sins of later life ; but Satan, as a skilled fisherman, knows how a small bait is better than a big one at first.

4. *All's fair in love and war and business.*—A miserable salve to an uneasy conscience! But has it any truth? There can be no love without respect, self-respect, and mutual respect, and how can these exist when anything and everything is justified whereby one gains his end? Is it true in war? Certainly not, as international agreements against explosive bullets show. In modern war

Commerical Morality Tending to Crime

Mercy has been recalled to the field whereon prisoners are made and the wounded lie; and if Mercy is not only allowed but bidden to be present, how much more must Justice appear on the scene? And what will Justice say as to anything and everything being fair? Very far gone then is he in dishonesty who would apply to business, *i.e.*, mutual exchange for mutual benefit, the adage discredited even in the face of the passions which love and war evoke. Reclaim the proverb from Satan to God, and let it stand, " Let all be fair in love, and war, and business, and so shall courtships, campaigns, and commerce all be purged of many a common evil and rise in the estimation of all."

5. *A man must live.*—How often with a depreciatory smile or a shrug of the shoulders do we hear this saying quoted as if all proverbs were the expression of Divine wisdom, and yet used to justify what no reason or equity can allow. Because proverbs are so frequently the condensation of a divine inspiration, and the portable property of the best wisdom or experience of a people, one may be sure that the powers of evil will adulterate, curtail, or parody them, and persuade men to take the counterfeit or the partial truth for the truth itself. Is this proverb true? Another one gives it the lie:

How Criminals are Made and Prevented

Fiat justitia ruat cœlum—Be just though crushed, expresses the right and manly view. Must one live? No, answered Horace, two thousand years ago—

> "The man of firm and righteous will,
>   No rabble, clamorous for the wrong,
> No tyrant's brow, whose frown may kill,
>   Can shake the strength that makes him strong.
> Should Nature's pillared frame give way,
>   That wreck would strike one fearless head."

The fact is that the proverb is an artfully curtailed one, and to any right-minded and clear-thinking man it runs thus: "A man must live rightly." Had he perforce to choose between life and integrity (not to descend to the choice between mere coin and conscience), by surrendering his life he will vindicate and exalt his integrity. It is the manner, and not the fact of life which counts.

6. *Honesty is the best policy.*—A sententious sentence invented by worldlings for worldlings, to be fairly met by the question: Is your dictum the result of your experience? have you tried both ways of action and find one preferable? No one who is honest will want it: few who are dishonest will be restrained by it. It is the adage and motive only of those who want to condemn others in order to

Commercial Morality Tending to Crime

extol themselves. It means for some, Let us, for this occasion, act as do others who habitually take honesty and not expediency as their rule. It is alike a truism and an untruth. A truism for those who are prepared to suffer loss rather than to inflict injury on others; who consider profit not as the gaining of a world but as the preservation of righteousness. And an untruth, for honesty which is the result of policy is not the habitual honesty that alone can claim the name. Truth is eternal and immutable: policy is fluctuating and temporal. The proverb denotes and pre-supposes a liberty of unblamable choice between what is wrong and right; expediency has no *locus standi*, its voice has no right to be heard, when such a choice is before us. It is curious that both the words, honesty and policy, are only found once in the Bible. It is worth while to quote the only use of the latter: " His policy shall cause craft to prosper." It is, moreover, obvious and indisputable that the principle of policy is condemned *passim in Scripturâ*, and that honesty is the precept of every page. Policy offered kingdoms to Christ. Honesty made Him refuse the proffer of Satan. Policy found a mouthpiece in Caiaphas and in Pilate: honesty brought Christ willingly to the Cross. Policy, said

How Criminals are Made and Prevented

the heathen Danes to our St. Edmund, King and Martyr, will lead you to extort your ransoms from the people, for "can we not kill you"? Honesty inspired his truly royal answer, "And can I not die?" So, when told we shall lose by our unconventional and scrupulous honesty, let us answer, And can we not lose? Or, when men are most threatened with derision for maintaining a higher standard than that usual in their trade or society, let them answer, Let them laugh!

All very well, men, and especially young people in their first place of business, are told; the parson is no doubt right in his own line, and you can listen to him on Sundays; but business and religion will not mix, and the axioms of business cannot be measured by the standard of religion. I agree: business and religion will not mix: but religion and business will mix very well. It all depends on which is first in your thoughts, chief as your mainspring of action. Listen to George Herbert :—

"Who is the honest man?
He that doth still and strongly good pursue,
To God, his neighbour, and himself most true:
Whom neither force nor fawning can
Unpin or wrench from giving all their due:

Commercial Morality Tending to Crime

> Whom none can work or woo
> To use in anything a trick or sleight,
> For above all things he abhors deceit.
> His words, and works, and fashion too,
> All of a piece: and all are clear and straight."

Let the business man commit these lines to memory. Let him write them on a card to be kept in his pocket-book. Let them hang up in his private office. So shall he and the world be better and fewer become criminals because of the initial degradation caused by the immoral morality of much commerce and many commercial men.

Tests of honesty are not difficult to imagine or to discover. For example, when a man is offered a "reward for his honesty" in restoring some valuable property that he has picked up, does he resent, as an insult that only ignorance or a low level of moral tone can excuse, the implied supposition that he might have acted otherwise? You imply some wonder that he should not have felt, or that he should have resisted, a strong temptation to keep what was not his own when you propose to pay him for virtue, and for doing to you as he would desire all men to do unto him. The pay of an artisan and that of thousands of the clergy is much the same: why would you never

How Criminals are Made and Prevented

think of offering one of the latter half a crown for restoring your lost book, and be somewhat surprised if the former did not accept it? Are you not in a certain degree proceeding on the assumptions that morality and probity belong mainly to certain classes, or that there are varying standards of honesty—which is as impossible as that there should be one law of purity or of temperance for the man and another for the woman?

Again. Cheat as you would be cheated; is that the revised version of Do as you would be done by? Commerce is but barter, and barter need not be in essence and intention far removed from the first love gifts of Adam and Eve before their fall—why do you propose to make it the bestowal of the bludgeon of Cain in return for the trust of Abel?—Or, let us honestly interpret " One must live." In how many hearts it means one must live in luxury, and therefore others must pinch and starve. One must live as Dives, and therefore Lazarus must shift for himself. One must consume without producing, careless of whether we freely cause others to produce without consuming. How cynical is the shrug, how reptilian the smile, with which this maxim is oft propounded! How selfish the heart from which alone it could spring!

Commercial Morality Tending to Crime

How unheroic and ungenerous the life based on a principle so mean! We hear these sayings, know their prevalence and force; how seldom as honest, brotherly men do we combat them with scorn!

This leads us to consider the large question of honesty in word. Familiar is the phraseology of the law-courts, " The evidence you shall give shall be the truth, the whole truth, and nothing but the truth," an adjuration which becomes an oath by the addition of the words "so help you God" and the kiss or uplifted hand of assent. Such an oath we know is no stimulus to the good man, no check to the bad one; but perhaps necessary or useful in view of the large intermediate class that is neither good nor bad. This oath reminds us that there are three forms of dishonesty in speech. There is first the downright lie, for which no one has a good word, and if it be possible to make it worse, there is perjury—the lie that has been immediately preceded by a solemn oath to tell the truth. Judges and magistrates have been lamenting recently that perjury is tremendously on the increase, much in the police courts, more in the county courts, most in the divorce court perhaps. Surely they have some power of bringing perjurers to book. Occasionally, but far too

How Criminals are Made and Prevented

rarely, this is done, and considering that the whole fabric of ordinary trust on which Society is built is shaken by the habit of perjury, some vigorous and sustained action on the part of those who hear and detect perjury is desirable. It would cram our prisons for a while, but the snake would soon be scotched if not killed.

Perjury remains as a serious matter in our Criminal Code, and involves penalties as heavy as righteous, but the cost of prosecutions, the uncertainty of success against one who has proved himself ingenious and versatile in his lying, and the fact that in some cases every one's business is no one's matter, lets perjurers, in ninety-nine cases out of a hundred, go scot-free. The magistrates have some power in the matter, and if more is needed they should seek it. "Perjury is committed before me in almost every case which I try in this Court," said the Recorder at the Old Bailey on November 5, 1912. And on November 6th, the Lord Chief Justice said in the "Old Masters" case, "The statements of the two parties were irreconcilable. . . . It was oath against oath, and it was one of the most painful cases of the kind he had ever had to try."

"Perjury is committed one hundred times a week

Commercial Morality Tending to Crime

in the City of London Court," remarked Judge Rentoul, at the Old Bailey, when counsel observed that perjury was not a common offence. His lordship added that men committed perjury in order to save paying about 1s. 6d., and in the case under notice the prisoner committed perjury to save a 5s. fine. Something must be done, he said, to prevent perjury, or there would be no object in the taking of an oath. In this case, exceptionally, the accused was sentenced to a month's imprisonment in the second division for committing perjury in the police-court. He was summoned for driving without a light, and swore he was nowhere near the place at the time.

Perjury, say the magistrates and judges, is rampant and increasing. Why should they not have power to commit at once for trial any witnesses who had, in their judgment, plainly perjured themselves from interested motives and to shield a crime? And when a case has become notorious by the time it has been before the public, if perjury is more than reasonably suspected on either side, surely this is a case which should, in the interests of public morality, be taken up by the Public Prosecutor, if neither of the contending parties has energy or money left. Men will often shrink

How Criminals are Made and Prevented

from the appearance of vindictiveness which would be involved in such a prosecution, especially when their reputation has been vindicated; but in the larger interest of the common weal the perjury should not be allowed to go unchallenged or unpunished. *Alibis* often break down utterly and are shown to be not merely a lie, but a concerted lie, and often, it may very reasonably be supposed, a suborned lie. That such persons should be awarded simply the punishment of not succeeding in their attempt to frustrate justice, is in itself an immorality and a crime against the State greater and of more far-reaching injury than that concerning which the perjury has been committed.

Nor is the half-truth to escape censure—Tennyson describes it as "ever the worst of lies." It is a dagger for our brother's heart, the handle of partial truth protecting, we hope, our assaulting hand from injury, while the blade of untruth can do its deadly work.

Then as to telling nothing but the truth, exaggeration in Society is regarded as an amiable vice at the worst; while in trade circulars and advertisements we presume its presence and discount the most positive assertions or figures of the advertiser.

Commercial Morality Tending to Crime

Then there is cant, the most repulsive form of all dishonest speech, and worst of all that cant which takes the garb of religion to conceal its lies, the cant that apparently pays by deceiving some innocents, according to the great use made of it by mendicants and many professedly religious persons whose names are to be found on the Cautionary Lists of *Truth* or of the Charity Organization Society. But be it remembered that many of those who talk about the cant of religious professors are in the habit of using cant of their own. There is the cant of pseudo-philosophy, or of Society, or of journalism, as much as that which is a parasite on religion. When the professional critics and reviewers of plays and novels will not say "Here is dirt," but ring the changes on "French," or "risky," or "daring," they are not only canting but are mighty factors in the pollution of minds and the depravation of life by their glossing over what is dirty and polluting to those who read books or see plays from which they would have been warned away by honest critics. I am often reminded, when I hear people talking about cant, of the story of Plato, who, when Diogenes found him in a gorgeous room with splendid carpets, and said, "I trample on the ostentation

How Criminals are Made and Prevented

of Plato," said, "Yes, with an ostentation of your own."

And here is a matter which goes to the root and origin of much immorality and crime, the honest man will give the right name to things and call a spade a spade. If we go back to "the pure well of English undefiled," the Bible, there is no doubt about a spade being called a spade therein. You find, for example, "drunk" and "drunkard," "harlot" and "whoremonger," but not the popular, grotesque, or inane terms whereby fools are led to make a mock at sin. If our friend was drunk, and we must tell him of it, then let us say so, and by the ugly word perhaps help to save him from an ugly habit. Why should we go to the thieves' kitchen or to the gutter for one of the two hundred slang terms which mean "drunk," but have not the honesty to say so? So with the sister sin of impurity. Terribly is it fostered and promoted by light terms for a heavy matter. A "gay" woman is a woman who can never be gay while the lie-name can be ascribed to her, whatever may be her forced giggles and artificial shrieks of laughter. A picture sermon by John Leech in *Punch*—a true moralist truly gay—might well teach us saving honesty instead damning dishonesty of speech. Two

Commercial Morality Tending to Crime

girls meet on Waterloo Bridge (the Bridge of Sighs to many) on a drizzling night, ragged, thin, with hectic cheeks. They have not met since, maybe, they sang side by side in a village choir, and one says, "Oh, Alice, how long have you been gay?" "Gay!" Nor could the sermon of an old lady be forgotten by its hearers, when in a West End drawing-room she heard some ladies discussing the habits and appearance of some " pretty horse-breaker," which was a slang term when I was a lad. "Excuse me, my dears," said she, "do you mean a harlot?" Stern was the word, but loving, too, for them, if they had wit and seriousness to perceive it. " One more unfortunate." Charity has, no doubt, been promoted by Hood's line; but also the sense of sin has been obscured and almost obliterated by it in those who seek in a way to regard themselves as will-less automata, as victims of misfortune which could neither be foreseen nor prevented. It is true, but not the whole truth, nor nothing but the truth. Our penny-a-liners have much to answer for, not only for what they report, but for the phrases in which they report it. The suicide, the theft, or quarrel in a house of ill-fame might best be left unreported; but if publicity is necessary, then the aim should

How Criminals are Made and Prevented

be to show that the way of transgressors is hard, or to plead for a less hard judgment on the part of society, or to combine the two aims. But neither aim exists in such a stereotyped expression as "living under the protection of a friend," which should be printed "under the protection (!) of a friend (!)." A duel has ceased to be called, at any rate in England, "an affair of honour," language in this instance ceasing to lie; and "debts of honour" should not be a term still applied to those which least are such. In defiance of reason and conscience I have infected myself with the fever of the gambler; another, possibly a swindler to boot, has prayed the blasphemous parody, "Give me this day my brother's bread, without my giving value in return," has gained the money which I can ill-afford to lose, and then this is a debt of honour! Whose honour—his or mine? There is but one honourable debt, "Owe no man anything, but to love one another," and the " debt of honour " is so out of the domain of integrity that the law will not help to recover it, Language, said the cynical statesman, was given to conceal our thoughts. Button up your pockets in the presence of one who quotes and believes this. *Fœnum habet in cornu*, he is marked, self-branded, as a social danger. True,

Commercial Morality Tending to Crime

some thoughts need much concealing; but it is only when the polluted brook has become a sewer that it needs a cover. Once it revealed its bed and reflected every flower.

After speech we come to deed, and herein especially to honesty in trading, or honesty as it affects all of us in our various capacities as having something to sell or a desire to buy something. At once we are met by the terrible fact that dishonesty in business, short of explicit theft, is considered by some to be inevitable. Said the Bishop of Lincoln lately: "It seems to me as if we were rapidly drifting into a condition of things similar to that in which the Church of Christ found itself in the first three centuries in the midst of the Roman Empire and surrounded by diverse and alien standards of morality and life." A sermon by the late Hon. and Rev. W. H. Lyttelton on "The Sins of Trade and Business," has bound up with it an essay by Herbert Spencer on "The Morals of Trade." From the latter writer I quote: "In tones of disgust or disparagement, reprehension or derision, according to their several natures" (characters, I suppose, he means) "men in business have, one after another, expressed or implied their belief that trade is essentially corrupt, and success incompatible with strict

How Criminals are Made and Prevented

integrity." The business of the moralist is to deny the necessity of this position; of his hearers to prove its falsity. Again he says: "To live in the commercial world, it appears necessary to adopt its code of morals, neither exceeding nor falling short of it. Those who sink below its standard are expelled, while those who rise above it are either pulled down or ruined." How saddening to think that to commercial morality in the present day should be applied a standard quite contrary to that which obtains to that of ordinary life. The loss of money is not that which most affects the moralist when he is swindled. Sad it is if we think it necessary to believe in the existence of such a low standard; sadder if we have experience of its commonness; saddest if we come to think we ourselves may or must act upon its lines. Yet one who was not only a statesman but also a successful trader—John Bright—wrote in answer to the question, Can a man be strictly honest in trade? that he "had heard of trades in which honesty is at a serious disadvantage; but he knew many who prospered because of their honesty. Character is capital to them, and balances or even exceeds dishonest gains that might be made."

But let us see if there is ground for the common

Commercial Morality Tending to Crime

idea that there is much dishonesty in trade, whether in production or in distribution.

With regard to production, few more sickening things can be read than the "Report of The Commission of Parliament on Adulteration." The only word for it is that it is simply an awful revelation of that to which greed and the haste to be rich can degrade men. There is not a trade in the land free from this disgrace; hardly an article to be purchased that was not found to be frequently adulterated. A very eminent London analyst wrote once to me: "It makes me very sorrowful to think we are such a bad lot. The indefiniteness of teaching has much to answer for. Thou shalt not steal is broader than it looks." "Blind names," *i.e.*, fictitious business names, are not unknown, in spite of recent legislation. Cigars made in Westphalia, shipped to London, are here marked as Havannah. Eleven shillings a hundred in Westphalia, delivered in London for 18s. 1d. duty paid, and fetching 60s. to 70s. wholesale as Havannah! This was, and may be still, the case. Buy silk or cotton, you find it loaded or mixed with inferior materials; you are the victim of a lie when the article is described, of a robbery when it is sold. Even savages have found us out and will have none

How Criminals are Made and Prevented

of our Manchester goods or the wares of Birmingham, which city has added to our language a new name for fraudulent inferiority. And then the very men who depress commercial morality complain of the natural and even righteous result, the depression of commercial prosperity, and, what is more to my present purpose, start every lad in their employ on a path that may lead to other forms of dishonesty. The poor man pays his pence for tobacco that is heavily watered and for beer of which the same may be said, and his wife buys what Chinese merchants have sent over with the strangely honest name of lie-tea, renamed by the English trader to the detriment alike of his conscience and his customer. Not only do we get bosh for butter, shoddy for cloth, and wine which has never been within a hundred miles of a vineyard, but this commercial habit produces such a state of mind that the milk-seller, mainly Welsh in London, will sophisticate or adulterate that on which the health and vigour and even the life of the infant or the consumptive or typhoid patient must depend, while the manufacturer will become careless of the even murderous results of his nefarious arts. I remember how in the East End many infants died because a scoundrel had adulterated his violet

Commercial Morality Tending to Crime

powder with a cheaper dust that was poison. And if sausages are "bags of mystery," jams are often "jars of fraud." Mr. Holmes, a Trades Council member, deposed that no textile goods required more than 25 per cent. of size, whereas he knew plenty of cases where 125 per cent. was used. Another member said he knew personally of instances of 200 per cent.; and a third drew attention to the terrible results of working ten hours in an atmosphere composed of steam and particles of China clay.

Or take the fur trade in which "faking" is largely practised. Cheap furs are dyed to imitate better furs. Among them are the following :—

Hare is described as foxaline.

Marten is described as imitation sable.

Rabbit becomes coney seal and electric seal.

Rabbit and *Hare* become imitation black fox, sable, and mink.

Racoon dyed becomes imitation skunk.

Nutria dyed becomes sealskin or beaver.

Red Canadian Fox dyed becomes black fox.

White Rabbit is treated to resemble ermine.

And surely something must be said as to excessive profit. Some would maintain there is no such thing; but this is not a doctrine they set

How Criminals are Made and Prevented

before their customers, and when they have challenged me for a definition of excessive profit my answer has been, That which you do not like to pay to others; and then they admit that a line should be drawn somewhere. It is fair and right that a man should make his living out of commerce; unfair and wrong that the buyer should strive to bid him down too far; but there must be a limit beyond which profit becomes iniquitous, and amounts to taking advantage of the ignorance or the necessity of a brother. Is it justifiable to sell for double the price that would leave you a good profit? Is it justifiable to make 100 per cent. profit? Would your customers buy if they knew the excessive difference between what you paid and what they are asked to pay? In two cases I traced profits. Penny bottles of ink were sold at 3s. 9d. a gross by the manufacturer. The sundries-man made a profit when he sold them at 4s., the traveller gained by selling them at 5s. 6d., and the shopkeeper netted more than 100 per cent. by his 12s. per gross. Is not the law of honesty somewhat strained by some one here? Another instance: I got a friend to inquire of a wholesale manufacturer of matches at what price they could supply him, and he found his profit would be 77 per cent. Of course

Commercial Morality Tending to Crime

we cannot, in the complexity of trade, lay down a hard and fast rule, but we need not therefore exclude all rules. Profits must vary according to the demand and the supply, the nature of the article, and so forth; but each who sells must make it clear to himself—to his conscience, not to his inclinations—that he can justify the particular profit he proposes. And each who buys cheap goods must be cognizant of the possible blood-guiltiness incurred by giving a price which cannot enable the maker to be properly paid.

Again, the question must be faced, What amount of interest for money is right, and what is excessive? Any gain for money lent was known, until comparatively recently, by the less comfortable name of usury. Of course, from the Christian and brotherly point of view it is not obvious why, if I am called upon and able and willing to lend a man £5, I should require any money in payment for its use—nor have I ever done so; and we should seek to extend those bounds within which natural affection would make the idea of interest an abhorrent thing. But, as Dr. Figgis says in his "Civilization at the Crossroads," "At this moment it is the ethic of Christianity which is more unpopular than its creed. It hinders the free development of the individual in regard to society,

How Criminals are Made and Prevented

or it is disliked as ascetic and unnatural in regard to the private life; and in business relations it is rejected on principle as mere sentimentalism." Usury has always and everywhere been condemned by the Catholic Church, and one of our English Canons or ecclesiastical laws, the 109th, enacts that "If any offend their brethren by usury, the churchwardens shall faithfully present such that they may be punished by the laws, and such shall not be admitted to Holy Communion until they be reformed." The historian Gibbon says that the most simple interest was condemned in the East and West by a host of Councils and Fathers and Casuists. It may well be that in our days, and in the present highly complex and artificial state of commerce, it would be impossible to return to the Elizabethan times when "old ten in the hundred" was Shakespeare's brand of opprobium for Shylock; but yet some line might be drawn, and the poor might be more adequately protected against the extortion of most money-lenders and loan offices; while, of course, those who profess an interest in the promotion of brotherhood will bring to its lowest limit the interest they require from their brothers. I remember a Jew being expelled from a Glasgow synagogue for receiving excessive

Commercial Morality Tending to Crime

interest, but normally neither religion nor law seems to think itself capable of making or enforcing ordinances of restraint.

Note other ways in which danger to integrity, and the first steps which lead to crime against property, are found. Take perquisites for example. How often a stepping-stone to theft; how often a mere euphemism for robbery. In vain does the pet name of "perks" try to persuade us of the innocence of the practice, when it has not been a matter of permission or agreement. How do the "picking and stealing" of the Catechism differ? The latter covers taking that which you know you may not take; the former taking that which you do not know you may. Have I been told that these things may be my perquisites? Shall I tell my employer I take them, or would it be more prudent, *i.e.*, more to my interests, to hold my tongue and assume the consent which as yet has neither been sought nor given? Or "makings" again. When a man boasts that his makings are equal to his takings, as a railway ticket-office clerk did once before his dishonesty in giving change was detected and punished, it is plain that "makings" unmake the man, and are another sorry euphemism for theft. The autobiography of a converted police superintendent, or

How Criminals are Made and Prevented

master of a workhouse, or estate agent, or chief foreman, or head domestic, would in some cases reveal the extent of the practice whereby the acknowledged pay, even when admitted to be liberal, is largely increased in unacknowledged and illicit ways. Rarely did those to whom a commission was offered, (before the Illicit Commission Act at any rate) offered secretly, and coming in the issue out of the pockets of their employers, exclaim with Poobah in "The Mikado," "Another insult!" Rarely did they not follow him in saying, "I pocket it."

Next as regards dishonesty in distribution. Consider the miserableness of the necessity of the L.C.C. protecting us, especially the poor, and even the poorest in receipt of out-relief, from robbery in the matter of weights and measures. In 1895, the L.C.C. found that one out of every eleven weights or measures on stalls and barrows was incorrect, and one in twenty-five in shops. Two hundred and seventy-seven proceedings resulted in 251 convictions, and one must regret that fines only amounted to £264—a quite inadequate and undeterrent sum when it is considered how long the dishonest gain on every transaction may have been made before detection. Coal-merchants were as jealous of the Homeric

Commercial Morality Tending to Crime

epithet of "respectable" as publicans, but yet only by the action of the L.C.C. were some of them made honest, and one who is, and not one who has been made, honest, is alone worthy of respect. When the crusade was begun in 1890 injustice and robbery was punished in 444 discovered cases: next year, convictions dropped to 205; next year to 162; next to 82. In one single transaction four distinct dishonest profits were made in addition to that which was lawful, by (1) the coals being wetted and so made heavier, (2) the weights being false, (3) the sacks not being properly filled, and (4) an empty sack or two being taken in the waggon to be counted as having been emptied! To such spake Amos the Prophet, a forth-teller in the name of God, "O ye that swallow up the needy, even to make the poor of the land to fail . . . making the ephah" (by which men sold) "small, the shekel" (by which they received payment) "great, and falsifying the balances by deceit . . . yea, and sell refuse for wheat—the Lord hath sworn, Surely I will never forget any of their works."

And advertisements; who believes them? "As a rule," said a grocer to me, "I throw trade circulars on the fire," and if traders lie even to fellow-traders, why must we believe that they tell the truth always

How Criminals are Made and Prevented

to the more ignorant public. Not all the newspapers which claim it can have the largest circulation. Not invariably has the War Office done anything to cause the sale of "the property of an officer ordered abroad." Not always is either the adjective or the substantive justified in the "amazing sacrifice" of the draper's window. Nor is what you purchase in the shop always the same in quality as that which attracted you in front. The pirating of trade-marks again is reduced to such a fine art that, common as it is, the finest meshes of special laws seem unable sometimes to involve the trader who is thus dishonest.

Think next for a moment of the guilt of complicity in the dishonesty of others. How terribly common it is for employers to induce, and practically to force, employees to lie to and deceive the public under penalty of losing favour or promotion, or even employment, is well known to those to whom shop-assistants and clerks come with their cases of conscience. Other things besides kissing go by favour, and those are not in favour, although secretly respected, whose conscientious refusal has shamed the unconscientious suggestion or order. In thousands of cases, religious principles having been thus outraged by employers, the practice of

Commercial Morality Tending to Crime

religion seems an hypocrisy, and is deserted in spite of early training and previous habit, and then, if the clerk or shop-girl eventually dips into the till the employer who has made this possible poses as an injured innocent and prosecutes! No doubt, the young man or woman should defy the fear of consequences, and have the thought in the heart, if not the words on the lips, "How can I do this great wickedness and sin against God?" No doubt all, and not merely some, when they say to me "What will happen if I get the sack?" might accept my answer, "God will fill it."

No doubt the acquiescence is weakness, and a practical repetition of Judas's "What will you give me and I will betray Him unto you?" But still the fear is natural, when favour is valuable, promotion slow, and a new situation hard to find at once. When Adam Smith declared that "it is the workman's or the producer's fear of losing his customers which restrains his frauds and corrects his negligence," he had not a high idea of commercial probity! Can we wonder if those in authority can work upon the fears of those under them and make them instruments of deception? Hard, but not impossible; hard, and therefore to be attempted; is it to refuse to sacrifice

How Criminals are Made and Prevented

honour. To get on, to get honour, to keep honest, should be the guiding maxim of the young in commerce; but is it normally? And if not, why not? *Cui culpa?* Where honesty is not the starting-point and the goal, the getting-on will be in a downward direction, and dishonour is felt within, if not eventually displayed. In the life of Samuel Morley we read, " The prosperity of the firm was due to the principles upon which the business was conducted. They were all men of high principle and inflexible integrity; no trick or artifice would be tolerated by them. Their word was as good as their bond. Men knew that amid all the fluctuations of trade, amid its ever-varying temptations to falsify goods, to make the worse appear the better article, they would hold fast their integrity." A friend of mine, now a brother Canon, was a clerk in a wine-merchant's office. A customer complained in writing of wine being inferior to that last supplied. " Tell him," said the merchant, " it was out of the same bin." " I cannot," said my friend; " it is not true." The merchant stormed and talked of the sack, but was constrained to respect the virtue he would not practise, and no evil consequences followed to the clerk. It is just when a man determines to do

Commercial Morality Tending to Crime

right and take the consequences, that the consequences are not those that he dreads; or, if they are, they bring with them compensations that far outweigh the immediate and apparent loss. A domestic parable comes to me as I write. My granddaughter, aged five, was bitten by a dog, and "had eight holes," as she said. But so many consolatory presents came to her that she inquired, "Auntie Dora, don't you wish you had a bited leg?"

Sometimes the pressure comes from below instead of from above, as when manufacturers are forced (as they think or pretend) by tradesmen to supply goods marked of a greater length or width than is the case. Or customers, by the habitual demand for an abatement of price, more than suggest to sellers to mark their goods above their proper value. Those, too, who will have long credit both grind the faces of their poorer brethren (*quorum pars sum*) who pay cash, and almost oblige the trader to make and get money anyhow so as to carry on, in spite of the financial disadvantages of the credit system. "Be not partaker in another man's sin," is a text on which all should meditate, even when not convicted or conscious of the same form of sin in them-

How Criminals are Made and Prevented

selves. Honest a man may be, and yet not free from helping others to be dishonest. Perhaps by silence when he should speak. The servant, the workman, the clerk sees some trick played, some purloining, some waste, to the disadvantage of the employer. "I wasn't to know," he whispers to his conscience that suggests speech. "It wasn't my business to speak." Would he say that if he were to change places with his employer? "I couldn't round on him." Then may you not come under the condemnation of the Psalmist, " Thou sawest a thief and consentedst unto him"?

A word must be added here as to the curious idea that dishonesty against a corporate body is more venial than if it were against an individual. The injury is less personal, but no less personal is the sin. Yet it is said that if income-tax returns were honestly made no other tax would be necessary. And railways find it pay to employ many inspectors to detect those who would scorn to cheat a man, but do not mind cheating a company. One year the G.P.O. is said to have netted £10,000 by a raid on letters that should not have been dispatched bearing a halfpenny stamp as if they contained nothing of the nature of a letter. And how hard it was to convince our grand-parents

Commercial Morality Tending to Crime

that smuggling was theft. The result of keeping two consciences in this fashion can only be that we become double-minded.

Each class, each kind of trade or occupation, has its own specific temptation. Who can cast the stone? Says Herbert Spencer, "There is no reason for assuming that the trading classes are intrinsically worse than other classes. Men taken at random from higher and lower ranks would, most likely, if similarly circumstanced, do much the same. Indeed the mercantile world might well recriminate. Is it a solicitor who comments on their misdoings? They may quickly silence him by referring to the countless dark stains on the reputation of his fraternity. Is it a barrister? His frequent practice of putting in pleas which he knows are not valid and his established habit of taking fees for what he does not perform, make his criticism somewhat suicidal. Does the condemnation come through the Press? The condemned may remind those who write of the fact that it is not quite honest to utter a positive verdict on a book merely glanced through; or to pen glowing eulogies on the mediocre work of a friend while slighting that of an enemy; and may further ask whether those who, at the

How Criminals are Made and Prevented

dictation of an employer, write what they disbelieve, are not guilty of the serious offence of adulterating public opinion." And I would add, as a cleric, that the clergy are not unknown who scamp their work, or give but short measure for the amount of pay or position and regard they receive; while, as an author, I might (with no reference to the issue of this book) recall the remark, "Now, Barabbas was a publisher." Is it, again, the politician who would legislate against commercial immorality? But political morality, whether before or after election, is almost a match for that of commerce, without many of the excuses the latter can urge. And what is ever the tendency of party government, the evils of which are perhaps most patent in America, but to the development of that which makes but a few on either side of the House to be acknowledged as undoubtedly honest statesmen? Who can cast the stone? No single class; but yet the honest in all. Says Ruskin, "The acquisition of wealth is finally possible only under certain moral conditions of Society, of which quite the first is a belief in the existence, and even, for practical purposes, the attainability of honesty." Each trade, occupation, profession, has its own specific

Commercial Morality Tending to Crime

temptations, its own dishonest tricks. Let parents find them out, and by forewarning forearm their children before they enter into this walk of life. And, if some seem to have more than others, then, as John Bright said, "Parents may wisely consider this when looking out for employment for sons, and seek that trade which offers the least possible temptation."

Rerum cognoscere causas is one of the powers of man that lifts him above the beasts, and makes a difference between reason and instinct. Both men and beasts observe facts, and notice present conditions; man to a higher degree than beasts feels the necessity of tracing facts and experiences to some previous cause. Many are the causes of commercial immorality. Nothing is so simple as to have but one cause. Amongst the minor causes which incline men to the dangerous haste to be made rich, or to the carelessness as to whether money is made in creditable ways, are (1) the credulity of customers; (2) the greediness of purchasers, who want things at less than their fair value; (3) the increased difficulty in obtaining a living, which arises from the increased population and its being massed in certain places; (4) the increase of competition and the consequent cutting

How Criminals are Made and Prevented

of prices; (5) the higher standard of education, which causes, in the middle classes, a greater expense in bringing up a family.

But chief—most radical, most potent—is the intense desire for money: in a word, covetousness. Covetousness is often considered as out of place in the Decalogue, as obviously less, as more venial, than the previously enumerated sins and crimes of murder, adultery, theft, and perjury. It seems to some almost thrown in as a make-weight, or added merely to make an even number. But, on consideration, it will be found to be the last, as the stone which completes the spire, as the clenching nail. Keep the first and the last Commandments, and the rest will keep themselves. Free from covetousness, you will not rob your neighbour of property or wife, which you have schooled yourself not to desire. Acts are the result of motives and desires. If you "begin not to say within yourself" what is evil, you will not go on to do or to say what is evil. "Only covetousness," says one who would salve his conscience; yet "only" covetousness produced the worst character in the Old Testament, Balaam, and the worst in the New, Judas. Covetousness is plainly the foundation of all sins of trade, whether

Commercial Morality Tending to Crime

on the part of the buyer or the seller. "If any that is called a brother," says St. Paul to the Corinthian Christians, "or an extortioner" (and what if he be both? the second because the first? the rack-renter or the sweater, because a pecuniary glutton?) "with such an one, no not to eat." Not that all money-making implies necessary covetousness. Nor that carefulness about one's money is covetousness. But when money-making is the principal or ruling motive of life, or when things indefensible before the judgment-seat of conscience are done to gain money, then covetousness is found and cannot be denied. Riches may come with innocence, even with honour; but in the haste to be made rich, in the consequent adoption of the shady short-cuts to gain or affluence, rather than the slow and toilsome progress in the path of honourable industry, is danger, is temptation, is the welcoming of the occasions of sin. Our fathers made money slowly but honourably; their sons would make it quickly, even if dishonourably. This is the plain English of the thought which shame keeps unexpressed, yet does not repress.

We may not exclude commerce from the kingdom of morality, nor grant it an exemption from

How Criminals are Made and Prevented

the duty of moral improvement. Older political economy saw in trade an economic machine, the blind and callous force of which men could not control; which had no more to do with duty or character or moral sentiment than a windmill or a hairbrush. Our generation has known two newer schools, one of which only varies the error of the old in thinking that all will be right if only the machine belongs to the nation instead of to individuals; while the other maintains that the spirit of brotherhood must be evoked and applied in gross and in detail. The one stunned and stuffed us with "Supply and Demand"; the other is instant with its "Sirs, ye are brethren." Economic laws are not imperatives, but observations or statements of tendencies; the imperatives which these tendencies require are supplied by moral teaching. Commerce by itself would know only a metallic basis, and uphold but a single standard of success. Wedded, however, to morality, it seeks and treasures the wealth of the conscience and the wealth of the heart, not merely that of the mine, and covets what brings out good rather than what brings in gold. The individualist pleads, "My business is my private concern; what right has any one or anything else to guide or control

Commercial Morality Tending to Crime

it?" The Socialist answers "That cannot be a private concern which supplies or serves the public: if you will not be hand-led by right, you must be handcuffed by law."

But covetousness is not only a cause, but has its own causes. What are they? Many, no doubt. Let us indicate but two:

1. The indiscriminate respect paid to "wealth." A common phrase at the beginning of biographies used to be "born of poor but honest parents," as if it were remarkable and unusual for the unrich to be worthy of respect. Let us hope we have heard the last of this insult and injustice; but still the ill-clad boy, with little pocket-money, is taught at many a school by snobbish school-fellows that poverty is a contemptible thing; while a little later in life any early lessons of the nobility of integrity and self-denial and self-sacrifice "fade as a dream when one awaketh" in the stress and atmosphere of business life. Slowly, too, are property qualifications for even the primal rights of citizenship dying out, utterly noxious as they were and injurious in many ways. When I was first elected to a Board of Health a tradesman could give me six votes and an artisan only one. Still has England, and even more republican America, need to pray,

How Criminals are Made and Prevented

From the worship of millionaires, good Lord, deliver us. Still is the rotund ideal of the money-bag surrounded by worshippers who never see the necessity of asking, and of demanding an answer to the preliminary questions, How was this money made? How is it being used? Immorality (in all but the sexual sense of the word) may have been practised to gain this worship, and then increased immorality to maintain and increase the bloated condition of the idol and the number of its parasites and devotees; but the glitter of the gold, the rustle of the notes, blinds and deafens men. Privately, indeed, men may speak with contempt of the dishonestly successful, but their public reprobation will be reserved for the knave who is unsuccessful. The tremendous power for evil or for good that lies in the visible and audible expression of social opinion must be educated, encouraged, and used for the right. Let homage be given unstintingly, without jealousy, cavil, or insinuation, to the social benefactor who has gained and used rightly his money, and then a wholesome stimulus is given to industry and to the distributive propensity; but if given also to malefactors, corruption is fostered.

2. The love of luxury. Christianity, brotherhood, altruism, socialism, all say, How can we

Commercial Morality Tending to Crime

wallow in luxury when Lazarus lies at our gates? Luxury is no doubt difficult to define, to expose, and to prevent, for (1) it is a sin of general habit and not of one particular act. In a house, in a feast, in costume, it may be clear that luxury is the normal state, the congenial pursuit, without any one item suggesting profligate expense. (2) It is a relative, and not a positive, sin, for what is luxury to one rank or age may not be a luxury, may almost be necessities to another. Stockings, coffins, tea, tomatoes, have all been luxuries once. The duke, the merchant, the cook, the artisan, the factory girl, all may, and frequently do, fall into the sin of luxury, but in very different ways. (3) It is not condemned, it is even defended, by the common voice of the world. "It is good for trade" is the popular cant, the uneconomic delusion, by which vulgar, or profligate, or plainly noxious expenditure is often excused. Yet De Lavelaye, the French economist, rightly said, "Luxury sustains a state only as the cord sustains a man who is hanged—from a moral and economic point of view it is equally bad for the individual and for the community." But difficulty of definition should only invite us to define. Luxury is the living to self, is self-indulgence. It is making "I like it" our domi-

How Criminals are Made and Prevented

nant rule of life. It is usually a form of sensuality. It is the state of the gorged alligator, not that of the man who labours, not that he may labour no more, but in order that he may have wherewith to supply the deficiency of others. Some may be called to pass the mean in the direction of asceticism; but none by any right motive to transgress the line into the fat field of luxury. Luxury blinds us to the needs of our brethren, it increases our wants, and simultaneously decreases our power and our desire to help others or not to take advantage of men. It is not poverty, but by living beyond one's means through luxury, that leads to commercial immorality in the worst and most flagrant cases.

Are ugly ways, especially in commerce, increasing or decreasing? That is a question that would be answered differently according to whether the answerer is naturally inclined to optimism and takes habitually a hopeful view of men and matter, or whether he is a pessimist. One might quote the revelations which caused recent Acts of Parliament bearing on bribery, fraud, and adulteration; the other might believe that the effect of those Acts had prevailed to check the dishonest. Again, while personal observation or experience has not opened our eyes to the extent of dishonest practices, of

Commercial Morality Tending to Crime

course we naturally believe the best and hope for the better; while, on the other hand, a few recent instances in which we ourselves have been cheated, or of deep sympathy with some whom we have found to be the victims of sweating, over-renting, or excessive hours, or bad conditions of labour would incline us to a too hasty generalization that "all men are liars," or knaves, or selfish.

There are certain things that would seem inevitably to make for the increase of the evil, such as the undoubted increase of competition in all departments of commerce and of labour, and again the love of ostentation which we notice so much (largely through the unnecessary and undesirable attention drawn by the Press to the prodigal and inane expenditure of the over-rich), that we imagine that all our forefathers must have lived more simply. But, on the other hand, the greater attention which is happily paid to social absurdities and evils, even though it be by a handful of people; the readiness with which some organs of public opinion will allow social evils to be exposed and denounced; and the newer legislation which brings more and more social sins into the list of public and punishable crimes, these would tend to make evil appear more prevalent, simply because it was more apprehended

How Criminals are Made and Prevented

and reprehended. Before trade unionism was a power, before recent legislation as to factory inspection and regulations as to the conditions of labour, before the more universal and thorough working of the Acts repressing adulteration, no doubt wrongs flourished that now only manage to exist. And, certainly, when we read of the times when government habitually debased the coinage for gain, when tradesmen commonly kept a bag of base coin to be passed to the unwary or ignorant, and when national sympathy with the weak was so hard to create, as the agitation against the slave traffic showed in its inception, we may be inclined to believe that the standard of righteousness must have been generally lower. Perhaps the truth is that great and direct frauds and injustices have decreased, while small and less direct wrongs have increased from the greater complexity of social relations and the greater stress of life. Yet there is hope in the undoubted growth of the ideas of sympathy and brotherhood, before which direct and gross injury to the feeble must continue to decrease, from the elevation of public opinion and the consequent improvement and application of law. But the point remains, Why are we still so bad? Are there no remedies which might be applied, none others that can be

Commercial Morality Tending to Crime

sought and found? It seems to me there are. Of course, a fool or a knave will only see or plead the custom of the trade, the way of the world, the *vis inertiæ* of " It has always been so." But a man, worthy of that high name, will not simply note a custom, but will ask himself whether it be a good and honest custom ; and if it seems to him to make for unrighteousness, he will thereupon form two resolutions—first, not to acquiesce in or adopt it for himself, and secondly, to expose and to oppose it in the interests of others.

1. Something might be done by moral teachers convening conferences about commercial morality, in which the honest would be encouraged by finding themselves not alone as unsupported knights-errant, while the dishonest might be shamed into bringing their practice up to the level of their profession. Herein, also, tricks might be unveiled and safeguards suggested by those who had personal knowledge of both, and thus teachers would be taught how to teach more definitely. The tradesman will rarely acknowledge that tricks are common in his own trade—unless he has a new and pushing rival in his street—but he will be quite aware that other trades are not impeccable.

2. The increasing power of trade unions might

How Criminals are Made and Prevented

still more efficaciously be exercised against dubious or indubitably evil practices, and they would rise in general estimation when it was seen that they took higher ground than that of promoting what was only "the best policy," or of advancing merely what tended to the pecuniary advantage of their members. It has grieved me much when I have heard unionists defend the "ca' canny" system, which in its way is quite comparable to the intentions and acts of the sweater.

3. Systematic benevolence, begun in youth (I knew a solicitor who gave his children 5d. a week pocket-money because it was easier to know and to lay aside the tithe of 5d. than of 6d.) is a remedy that slays Goliath with his own sword. The habit of setting apart a definite proportion of salary, wages, pocket-money, extras, profits, windfalls, as not belonging to ourselves all, but to God and our neighbour, will be the constant and regular reminder of the claims of brotherhood and of religion, a periodic suggestion of self-sacrifice and generosity, a taking of the rudder of life out of the entire grasp of selfishness as the ruling power. The habit of thus tithing one's income—and I have known nobles, clerics, stockbrokers, tradesmen, domestic servants, and street-sellers who adopted this rule—

Commercial Morality Tending to Crime

the offering " each week as the Lord hath prospered you "; the thank-offering for success; will all make the probability of having in the time of repentance to pay conscience-money, or to make restitution, less conceivable. (A great deal more preaching of restitution as a part of repentance, even of its legal enforcement in case of fraud or robbery, is necessary; but of this more anon.)

4. Let the expulsive force of a new affection be advocated and tried as a cure for the inclination to haste in money-getting, or the carelessness as to how it is made. A source of weakness in the life of England is that the trading classes especially read so little, except their ledgers, and have so few hobbies. With the exception of chemists, who are in a way scientific or professional men, literature, art, science, or natural history, church work or chess, domestic handicraft or athleticism, is more likely to find a student or adherent in the policeman than in the pork-butcher, in the dustman than in the draper, in the gardener than the grocer, and in the porter rather than in the vendor of the synonymous beverage. Only a few comparatively, and these not always the best, will take up any work of private or public benefit to others whether in municipal or in church work. It is of the

How Criminals are Made and Prevented

bourgeois that one most easily despairs as a class. If only they would commonly be something else besides traders, the atmosphere in which they live would be glorified as well as purified, commercial morality would cease to be the subject for jibes and flouts and sneers, and the traders would be the backbone of the nation's life. The bourgeois spirit is commonly harmful in civic life from its contracted views and the habit of the concentration of thought on money-making alone. Everything is weighed-up as "good for trade," or the contrary, and no amount of future benefit to the community, and still less of benefit to classes other than that to which they themselves belong, will counterbalance the desirability of "keeping the rates down." Absorption in personal or class interest is, of course, not peculiar to any one class, but it seems far more common amongst men of commerce than men of toil.

5. And let men have the courage and the manliness to be poor, to be contented with and even proud of poverty, if it be necessary for the retention of clean hands. So Nehemiah says: "Former governors were chargeable unto the people, and had taken of them bread and wine, beside forty shekels of silver—but so did not I, because of the

Commercial Morality Tending to Crime

fear of God." He would have been richer and more powerful if only he had been less moral and honest. Taking commercial men on their own ground, and using their own habitual meteyard, Christ inquires, what shall it profit a man if he gain the whole world—and lose his own soul?

It may be interesting and helpful here to see how ancient are the sins and the difficulties we have noticed: how ancient, also, and how little out of date are moral codes and catechisms. Let us study the Psalter and discover what may be called—

THE MORAL CODE OF DAVID.

Morality, religion, worship, commonly represent consecutive and progressive stages in the life of a nation or an individual, and we may discern these steps in the Psalter. With the exception of Psa. xlvii, in the first book we find little, when and because the Temple as yet was not, comparable to the sustained and irrepressible Alleluias of the last book. The earlier psalms are subjective, the later objective. The precepts of morality, their foundations, and the effect whether of their observance or of their neglect; the voice of personal experience whether in joy or sorrow, in danger or in deliver-

How Criminals are Made and Prevented

ance; and that expression of personal religion which makes the Psalms the book of devotion for all time; these are on the whole more in evidence in the first book, more characteristic of what David feels himself inspired to teach, than in the subsequent utterances whether of David or his successors before and after the Captivity.

I think it may be well to examine the first book as containing a moral code, and I write designedly away from the possibility of consulting any other commentary or exposition than is afforded by a comparison of our three translations, that of the Bishop's Bible which is retained in the Prayer-book for singing, and those of the Authorized and the Revised Versions.

It is significant that the Psalter begins with a benediction and ends with Alleluia. It is significant also from our present point of view that the opening benediction is for him who has been righteous or moral. The first verse of the First Psalm recapitulates the chief or usual causes of moral declension, and indicates that they are progressive. There is—

1. Following bad advice, though not habitually.
2. Frequent resort to bad company.
3. Deliberate choice of those who are aggressive

Commercial Morality Tending to Crime

in evil and contemn the righteousness which yet shames them.

This is shown by the successive verbs "walked," "stood," and "sat," and also by the order of the three words for the categories of the evil, "wicked" (A. and R.V.), "sinners" (B.B., A. and R.V.), and "scornful" (B.B., A. and R.V.).

Then in the twelfth verses we have the prophylactics against such causes of moral declension—

1. Delight in God's law.
2. Constant meditation on its precepts ("exercise" in B.B. becomes "meditate" in A. and R.V.).

Then in Psa. xv we find a definite catechism of morality.

Question in ver. 1 : " Lord, who shall sojourn and dwell with Thee?"— no occasional visitor, no temporizer.

Answer: " He that—

1. Walketh uprightly.
2. Worketh righteousness.
3. Speaketh truth in his heart.
4. Slandereth not with his tongue.
5. Nor doeth evil to his friend.
6. Nor taketh up a reproach against his neighbour.
7. In whose eyes a reprobate is despised.

How Criminals are Made and Prevented

8. He honoureth them that fear the Lord.
9. He sweareth to his own hurt, and changeth not.
10. He putteth not out his money to usury.
11. Nor taketh reward against the innocent."

Consequence and Reward (ver. 5).—"He that doeth these things" (observes this moral code) "shall never be moved." His practice of the Presence of God as an Inspirer of altruistic motives, will result in a fixity of abiding in His Presence here and hereafter.

N.B.—The chief change in the translations is from the "He that setteth not by himself, but is lowly in his own eyes" of the B.B., to the "In whose eyes a vile person is contemned" of the A.V., and the "In whose eyes a reprobate is despised" of the R.V.

Psalm xxiv gives us a second catechism of morality in a condensed form.

The question in ver. 3 asks: "Who shall live the ascending instead of the grovelling life?" Who shall rise up in the Holy place of the Lord, though not, maybe, in the estimation of his banker?

The answer is, "He that—
1. Hath clean hands,
2. And a pure heart;

Commercial Morality Tending to Crime

3. Who hath not lifted up his soul unto vanity,
4. And hath not sworn deceitfully."

Hands not defiled by ill-gotten gold, nor used to draw up lying trade circulars or advertisements or the prospectuses meant to deceive and entrap and despoil the ignorant brother. The heart not absorbed in getting that which will rust or be stolen here, and never be reckoned as wealth beyond the grave; the lips that despise "profitable" deceit, the cant of commerce, and the lies which pass for the justifiable maxims of trade. These are your requisites of manhood, these your keys to heaven.

Consequence and reward (ver. 5).—"He shall receive a blessing from the Lord, and righteousness from the God of his salvation."

This answer concisely summarizes that of the antecedent Psalm xv—Righteousness implies right works (1), right motives (2), right speech (4), and the despising of the world's standard (3). Therefore, comparing the extended and the summarized code (as a child is taught to extend the Decalogue in the Duty towards God and the Duty towards his Neighbour) we may note that under (1) of this Psalm is comprehended 1, 2, 5, 10, and 11 of Psalm xv; against (2) we may place 3; under (4)

How Criminals are Made and Prevented

we include 4, 6, and 9; and under (3) we place 7 and 8.

Psalm xxvi is a declaration of integrity (this word in A. and R.V. supplants the "innocency" of B.B.) after self-examination, which self-examination has obviously been based on Psa. i, with the result that David trusts that he has—

1. Not sat with vain persons,
2. Neither gone in with dissemblers.
3. Hated the congregation of evil-doers,
4. And will not sit with the wicked.

Here, again, notice the progress in the degrees of iniquity, the frivolous, the hypocrites, the evil-doers, and the habitually wicked.

So the declaration of the beginning of the Psalm, "I have walked in mine integrity," becomes the resolution of the end of the Psalm, "I will walk in mine integrity," and yet the weakness of will when not aided by grace is affirmed by the prayer appended to the resolution, "Redeem me, and be merciful unto me."

In Psa. xxxiv is the third moral catechism.

Question in ver. 12 : "What man is he that desireth life and loveth many days that he may see good?" (A. and R. V.)

Commercial Morality Tending to Crime

Answer: He who hears and obeys these precepts:

1. Keep thy tongue from evil,
2. and thy lips from speaking guile.
3. Depart from evil. But since a mere negative abstention from evil is insufficient, here are also—
4. Do good;
5. "Seek peace and" (which requires more resolution and perseverance when the angry or warlike spirit is aroused) "pursue it."

N.B.—St. Peter had no doubt about this being a moral code, nor of its value, for he quotes it *literatim* (perhaps as from the catechism of his boyhood), and urges its importance on his converts as the climax of his summary ("Finally, my brethren") of moral duties in 1 St. Pet. iii, 10.

Notice also that of these five Davidic and Petrine rules of life two, and the first two, refer exclusively to sins of word; and that the rest for many would concern the tongue chiefly, *i.e.*, *Depart* from the habit of lying, cursing, boasting; *Do good* by resuming prayer and lifting up your voice again in common worship; and *Seek peace*, not merely abstaining from being a cause of strife by angry or malicious words, but also making

How Criminals are Made and Prevented

opportunities of pacification and arbitration, *and pursue* peace without being rebuffed by initial or even repeated failure. *Beati pacifici. Magna est pax et prævalebit.*

Psalm xxxvi.—David, meditating on the characteristics of him who has abandoned the moral code sees that the primary cause is, "There is no fear of God before his eyes," but personal pleasure, and especially personal profit, have become his substituted god. Therefore, certain results follow:—

1. "He flattereth himself in his own eyes that his iniquity shall not be found out and be hated." What fools knaves are! will be the voice of those experienced in criminal matters.

2. "The words of his mouth are iniquity and deceit." All can testify to the prevalence of commercial immorality in trades other than their own, or as a reason for their rival's success.

3. "He hath left off to be wise and to do good." Cunning, Satan's parody of Divine Wisdom, has replaced the wisdom of which "the fear of the Lord is the beginning," and the middle, and the end. That once he knew better and did good makes his responsibility and his condemnation the greater.

4. "He deviseth iniquity upon his bed." Schem-

Commercial Morality Tending to Crime

ing for his personal profit has become an obsession with him, and vitiates his home and prevents or agitates his slumbers.

5. "He setteth himself in a way that is not good." Not "an occasional flutter" or "a questionable proceeding once in a way," but he has at last settled down into the cursed necessity of ill-doing.

6. "He abhorreth not evil." We rather regret the more didactic, if less accurate, translation of the B.B., "Neither doth he abhor any thing that is evil," which is more true to nature. "If you had told me once that I should ever do a thing of this sort," said a prisoner to me, "I would have kicked you!" "Quite right," said I. "Now try to get into such a state that you can again have a reason to kick."

In Psa. l, Asaph, or David "for Asaph," makes God convince of sin those who were still professing religion and yet resented rebuke and excused sin as the responsibility of others. "What hast thou to do to declare My statutes, or that thou shouldst take My covenant in thy mouth?" All the while—

1. "Thou hatest instruction." Note that the authors of the B.B. or Prayer-book version could

How Criminals are Made and Prevented

not resist the dishonest temptation to make ecclesiastical or political capital by the mistranslation, "Thou hatest to be reformed," when the Reformation wrangles were still clamant. An accurate and largely justified translation in our days might be "Thou pratest about real religion and thinkest thou canst never learn anything from sermons;" or "Thou dost delight in doctrinal sermons (if according to thy party or sects), but dost abuse those that speak plainly as to moral points."

2. "Thou castest My words behind thee," picking and choosing what words, precepts, or acts of Christ thou shalt approve and believe and imitate.

3. "When thou sawest a thief, thou consentedst with him," *e.g.*, by becoming a shareholder in a company whose high profits connote under-payment of labourers. A company may have "no soul to be saved, and no body to be kicked"—but its shareholders have both.

4. "Thou hast been partakers with adulterers," thy colleagues in the Houses of Parliament, thy companions in the clubs, those whose guilt thou pleasest to consider less than that of adulteresses; by defending publication of suggestive and provocative matter in thy paper, with the only

Commercial Morality Tending to Crime

excuse that it sells the paper and that rivals do the same.

5. "Thou givest thy mouth to evil." Think of the common conversation of the factory, or the smoke-room of the club or ocean steamer: or of electioneering speeches and placards, withdrawn only when their dirty work has been done: all without thy rebuke, even if not with thy aid.

6. "Thy tongue frameth deceit." And as this particular denunciation is addressed to religious professors, unreality in religious profession may be chiefly meant, the cant or slang of any religious party.

7. "Thou sittest and speakest against thy brother; thou slanderest thine own mother's son." What else is most of the religious controversy of the religious? Were not F. D. Maurice or Bishop King of Lincoln sons of thine own Mother, the Church of England? And who financed or approved their prosecution?

All this teaching, catechetical and otherwise, as to the moral code, we have found in the First, or Davidic, Book of the Psalms, and going through the subsequent one hundred, we find it not in such proportion. There is, indeed, Psa. ci, headed "A Psalm of David," in which there is a list of

How Criminals are Made and Prevented

the kinds of companions who will be avoided by the righteous man, the froward, the slanderer, the proud, the deceitful, the lying, and the workers of iniquity. There is Psa. cxii, the antithesis and the antidote to the puzzled and nearly despairing cry of Psa. lxxiii. There the difficulty was that "I do see the ungodly in such prosperity," and the answer was, "Wait and see; what is apparent and present is not always permanent or real"; but here the initial and sustained cry is that the righteous are and shall be blessed, and that the ungodly shall see, and it shall grieve him, . . . the desire of the ungodly shall perish. But, generally, the rest of the Psalter is made up of the voice of personal experience, of personal religion, of prayer, of confession, and of praise. It is David, the man of the comprehensively immoral act that is never forgotten, who is also David the moralist, David the interpreter of Moses the law-giver, David who shows that God's Commandments are exceeding broad and that the Decalogue is not simply the condemnation of ten sins or crimes which in the letter, as regards some of them at any rate, most can say "I have not transgressed Thy law," or, "All these have I kept from my youth up": David, who shows that religion must be concerned

Commercial Morality Tending to Crime

with particulars and not simply with generalities. David, whose moral code has been the one great source of most subsequent moral systems. For David, therefore, all prophets or forth-tellers and teachers of morality give thanks, and to the gad-flies who would settle on his one sore they point to his monumental moral code and precepts and warnings and encouragements; while even as to the one great lapse, there are the striking words of St. Augustine, " Most blessed sin of David, so gloriously atoned for," or St. Hildebert's "Ah! King of Israel, ah! ancestor of Christ, is not this of God's infinite mercy towards thee that since thou hast occasioned, and wilt occasion to the end of the world, so many and so horrible blasphemies, that thou shouldst also be the channel through whose words the grace of God has descended to so many penitents?" Men are too ready to remember the sin, too slow to remember the beauty and strength of the antecedent moral teaching and of the subsequent penitence shown in Psa. li.

Many read and quote the Bible as if the only virtue it inculcated was that of Faith. Few notice how much of its history and precepts is directed to the impressing on us of moral rather than spiritual duties, and how the duties of brotherhood and

How Criminals are Made and Prevented

citizenship are held up to us as a means of serving God in our generation as real as that of worship. Prophets are recognized as fore-tellers in the name and by the power of God; men fail to observe how more frequently they are forth-tellers, and their "Thus saith the Lord" refers to some present duty, political, civil, or sanitary; or, in the more definitely spiritual sphere of action, to the conviction of sin (an almost lost power in our generation, said Gladstone), the necessity of contrition, confession, and amendment, rather than to some future hope or promise.

Another point which commonly escapes notice is that when a portrait of the man after God's own heart, the man justified before Him, is given, the test of character is derived largely, or even chiefly, from his discharge of his duty to his neighbour. In the Psalter we have seen this portrait sketched in the form of a question with the answer given that includes rules for human conduct, such rules referring mainly to points of moral rectitude. Let us supplement this by later evidence, the striking passage in the thirty-third chapter of Isaiah. The fore-teller of the Incarnation and the Passion is here the forth-teller of how the new man is to be put on and the old man crucified, and to those who would

Commercial Morality Tending to Crime

hope for the Beatific Vision, not a life of ecstatic worship or unworldly meditation is propounded, but (as a preliminary, at any rate, to these—a foundation on which a superstructure may be reared) six very practical rules of life are given to guide him in the street, in the shop, in the law-court.

"Who among us shall dwell with the devouring fire? Who among us shall dwell with everlasting burnings?" is the question, unlike in form, but perhaps identical in import, with those already noted in the Psalter. No doubt to many the idea of that self-created state of loss and pain which we call Hell, is at once and exclusively suggested by the phrases, "devouring fire," and "everlasting burnings"; but more comprehensive thought will remind us that the image of fire is quite as often connected with the idea of Heaven as with that of its antithesis, as expressing in human language something of the nature and the manifestation of God Himself. "Our God is a God of fire." The presence of God expressed under this image is here and hereafter a joy to some, a torment to others, according to what they choose their conduct and character to be. Public worship to one is a tedious conventionality at best; to another in the same building a refreshment, an inspiration, an ennoblement.

How Criminals are Made and Prevented

The same whisper of conscience or holy inspiration is welcomed by one and resented by another. So the Vision even to the best is unsupportable (think of Moses on Sinai, the apostolic witnesses of the Transfiguration, Saul on his way to Damascus), without the training of a practice of the recollection of the Presence which renders even its veiled splendour, its afterglow, more bearable. A careful reading of the whole of this passage from Isaiah will serve to reveal the law that duty to one's neighbour is the test of duty towards God, and that moral conduct enables us the better to contemplate the possibility of being able to stand the Presence of the otherwise unsupportable glory. Who among us can face this fire? The answer gives the portrait of a man—not of a mere human being—of the *vir* and not just the *homo*. And the portrait is drawn in six strokes. Six rules of life give the scaffolding whereby shall be reared, according to the design of the Great Architect of the Universe, the tower of a manly, because godly, and godly because manly, life that shall stand foursquare to all the winds that blow—

1. "He that walketh righteously." He condescends to no tricks, whether of trade or of politics. He will not, because he cannot with the

Commercial Morality Tending to Crime

ideal in him and the hope before him, take a mean and murky advantage of the absence of an observing eye, whether of employer or customer, or wife, or moral teacher. Nor can he take advantage of the ignorance of any, for the upright walk constrains him to help and not to hinder his brother. No "guarantee for fidelity in business" is necessary for him.

2. "He speaketh uprightly." His word is his bond, and is speedily known as such. He takes the oath in law-courts, as he may also take the pledge of abstaining from alcohol, not as needful for himself but to enable him to aid the infirmity of others. Uprightly, also, he rebukes evil when met or heard, and thus avoids the complicity of silence. He can't cant. He confesses Christ before men, since else he finds no possibility of the uprightness that animates his acts whether for or before man or God.

3. "He despiseth the gain of oppressions." He dares not take, nor will stoop to make, excessive profit or the interest which becomes usury, for he sees therein his brother's loss rather than his own temporary and finally injurious gain. None of the meaner maxims of trade will he use to salve the conscience that stings and reproaches, when the

How Criminals are Made and Prevented

possibility of something underhand or over-reaching is momentarily presented. Not only short weights, lying placards, goods not up to sample, or too long hours of labour enforced, but also the Sunday shopping which enfeebles the body, clouds the mind, and burdens the conscience of those he makes to serve him, are to him despicable. He groans at the thought of how traders of his nation for gain stupefy with opium, or madden and exterminate with spirits, the tribes and nations with whom they deal.

4. "He shaketh his hand from holding of bribes." As St. Paul in Melita shook off the viper into the fire, so with a shudder that integrity has made instinctive, he abhors the purchase-money of iniquitous silence, or speech, or action, or inaction. As I write, comes an article in the *Daily News* on one of the characteristics of America, the home of divorce, and lynching, and bribery—

"Lieutenant Becker, of the New York police, has been found guilty of murder, and although New York opinion is not entirely satisfied with the manner in which the trial was conducted, nobody disputes that this affair has revealed, or rather illuminated, an alliance between sections of the New York police and the exploiters of vice of

Commercial Morality Tending to Crime

the most appalling character. A police force from the nature of things is always exposed to corruption. It is brought into the most direct contact with criminals, and the contact of hostility may in individual cases very readily pass into the contact of licence and co-operation. There have been instances enough in the history of the English police forces. But what is commonly believed to be occasional and sporadic over here is commonly believed in New York to be permanent, systematic, almost universal. Now it is impossible that if, for instance, we in London thought that the Metropolitan Police systematically co-operated with criminals the thing would be allowed to last. Public opinion would insist upon reform at all costs. But the people of New York have for many years been persuaded of the existence of a working alliance between their police and their criminals, and yet they have done nothing and tried to do nothing to sweep the evil thing away. Are we to conclude that the New Yorkers lack a real public opinion and a real civic spirit?"

Grant that in England statesmen and judges are not now bribable—at least in coin; grant that "every man has his price" is not now as true as once it appeared to be in many circles and stations;

How Criminals are Made and Prevented

yet Bribery Acts have been needful in recent years. "Don't tell mother and you shall play with my doll." "Don't let the master know and you shall have my knife." "Keep it dark, old fellow, and I'll make it worth your while." "I made it all right with the foreman"—how we know these voices proceeding from the shop, the school, and even the nursery. How can a child of the light "keep it dark"? Why should one make it all wrong with his conscience by "making it all right" with some one else?

5. "He stoppeth his ears from hearing of blood"—or even of knock-out blows, a "putting a man to sleep" in the prize ring. There is a beast within us that rejoices, as there is an angel within that shudders, at the very sound or suggestion of cruelty. "How sad," said Queen Victoria, "that there should be any need of a Society for the Prevention of Cruelty to Children." True; but the revelations of that Society are in volumes, and show how neither education nor the profession of religion is the bar it should be to the lust for cruelty which is sometimes the substitute for lust of another kind, and sometimes only its symptom and its incitement. Bull-baiting and cock-fighting are extinct; but who pretends that our lesser and

Commercial Morality Tending to Crime

weaker brethren need not still the protection of the Society for the Prevention of Cruelty to Animals? We may think that the clamour for the abolition of vivisection, of corporal punishment, of the death penalty, are not wholly justified; but even if exaggerated in aim as well as often in diction, they may be a necessary safeguard against a recrudescence of the savage element in our nature. It is not because the editors of professedly respectable papers believe in the desirability of stopping men's ears from the hearing of blood that they devote their columns, and the largest type of their contents bills, to the highly unnecessary details, or the halfpenny-catching advertisement, of the last awful murder.

6. "He shutteth his eyes from seeing evil." Here come the wretched newspapers again, and many of our playwrights and owners of theatres, making dirt more sticky in pursuit of gain, and offal more stinking by their canting and hypocritical defence of it, by the prostitution of the names of Literature and Art. As regards the evil done by newspaper reports of proceedings in the Divorce Court, it has been recognized from the first.

Shortly after divorce cases began to be published, a noble and characteristic protest was uttered by

How Criminals are Made and Prevented

Queen Victoria, who wrote on December 26, 1859: "The Queen wishes to ask the Lord Chancellor whether no steps can be taken to prevent the present publicity of the proceedings before the new Divorce Court. These cases, which must necessarily increase when the new law becomes more and more known, fill now almost daily a large proportion of the newspapers, and are of so scandalous a character that it makes it almost impossible for a paper to be trusted in the hands of a young lady or boy. None of the worst French novels, from which careful parents would try to protect their children, can be as bad as what is daily brought and laid upon the breakfast table of every educated family in England, and its effect must be most pernicious to the public morals of the country."

But Parliament threw its ægis over this source of corruption, for the Lord Chancellor, Lord Campbell, replied to the Queen that "having attempted in the last session to introduce a measure to give effect to the Queen's wish, and having been defeated, he was helpless to prevent the evil." So it continued until, a generation later, the Press printed, most of them, a protest of some hundred Members of Parliament against the publication, for

Commercial Morality Tending to Crime

no moral but much mercantile purpose, of utterly needless and plainly injurious details of divorce and other unsavoury cases; but when next some spicy or sensational copy could be made, the evil to which they opened their eyes was that of not selling so many copies as their rivals in journalism. As the *Athenæum* of October 26, 1912, says, "We have not forgotten the *Punch* cartoon depicting the dirty old man of the Press at the bottom of a pool of mud, offering to roll himself in it again for the sake of half-pence."

Or the novelists again.

The *Daily Mail* of November 8, 1912, said:—

"A few writers—mostly feminine—do gain an extensive circulation by novels which are prurient, suggestive, or frankly indecent. The promiscuous sale of these objectionable works is deplorable, though the question of limiting it is one for the police and the Legislature rather than for moralists and critics." On this comment, however, we may remark that if moralists held their tongue, public opinion would not make police action, and further, that if critics were more honest, and used the words "dirty" or "indecent" and not their beloved "risky" or "daring" the circulation would be confined to those who desired further to foul their

How Criminals are Made and Prevented

dirty minds, and the novels would not be found in reputable libraries or taken unknowingly into decent homes and hands. Not, of course, that the consumers of this garbage, this, at any rate, tainted food, are without their guilt, as well as the producers. Watch who or what are they who cluster round certain booksellers', stationers', and photographers' shops, and wonder if they ever knew or felt the importance of keeping a watch over their eyes, and of avoiding that in the paper or in the window which a momentary glance will show to be in the class of things which before have injured their minds or taken the bloom off their purity. If the two last tests of manhood voice the Sixth and Seventh Commandments, the breach of which is not a temptation to one class or occupation more than another, all the rest express the Eighth, Ninth, and Tenth Commandments, which especially regard the common dangers of those who buy, sell, or barter. But those who keep these rules before their eyes, who know them as the indispensable conditions of the upright life, what of them? Isaiah, who has been the forth-teller, now becomes the fore-teller with the gracious promise from God, "they shall see the King in His beauty" (they shall have, even now and here, some fore-gleam of the transforming

Commercial Morality Tending to Crime

inward vision of Christ and the Father by the power of the Holy Spirit within them) "and the land which is very far off," the land of glory and peace, of peace in men and towards men because first the glory of God has been sought. Our land, our world, hardly now corresponds to this name, even in shadow. Hood, recollecting how as a child he looked from his cot through the window, and thought that heaven, with its starry splendour, rested on the tops of the pine trees of the garden, wrote: "To me is little joy to think that heaven seems farther off than when I was a boy." Yet this world is salvable and transformable after all. Each can do his part, beginning at his own heart, whence light will radiate to an ever-increasing circumference.

Deformata reformare: reformata transformare: transformata conformare: to reform by repentance that which, by yielding to temptation from within or from without, has been deformed; by manly perseverance in well-doing to transform into a shape of greater beauty and light that which by grace has been reformed; and, finally, partly here, and more in Paradise, and most in the fire and everlasting splendour of "that perfect vision of God's Face which we, for lack of words, call

How Criminals are Made and Prevented

Heaven," to conform the life to the image of the Lord our Righteousness.

I said that we must recur more fully to the question of Restitution, partly because it is a necessary part of any repentance for a sin against honesty, and partly because its necessity is so commonly and so comfortably forgotten, and partly because this necessity is so little proclaimed and taught with definiteness and decision. In a paper read to the Central Committee of Discharged Prisoners' Aid Societies, my friend, the Rev. G. P. Merrick (first and late Chaplain-Inspector of H.M. Prisons) described it as a forgotten element in our penology, and pointed out that while the Civil Courts enforce some restitution or reparation in the shape of damages, the Criminal or Police Courts provide no such satisfaction for the injured party in the case of theft or fraud. To submit to loss and injury is often a less evil, it seems, than to incur the additional loss of time and money incident to a prosecution of the offender. Especially when the poor have been robbed magistrates would desire the power to enforce restitution, but they have no such power. As Mr. Merrick says: "Our present method thinks of little more than the

Commercial Morality Tending to Crime

infliction of a public penalty, and very little of the wrongs or rights of the private victim." Not thus acted the laws of Greece and Rome, to say nothing of the Levitical law. I suffer a loss by theft. The thief suffers financially not at all; but I have to suffer a second loss in the expense of prosecution, and a third in paying my share of his support in prison. This inclines the dishonest to ignore the idea of restitution, and the injured to be slow to invoke the aid of law.

With regard to its necessity as a part of repentance, it is sufficient to observe that by all law, whether natural, divine, or human, it is regarded as a precept of necessity, as being another form of the Eighth Commandment, which exists in all law. But, as the duty of restitution often arises from that which is a sin but no legal crime, it has to be the more noticed by theology as unnoticed by law. It is, in the words of Lord Clarendon, "an inseparable ingredient and effect of repentance." For, as St. Augustine wrote: "So long as that which was wrongly gained is not restored, if it can be restored, there is no act, but only a pretence, of repentance." Or, to quote Ezekiel, "If the wicked restore the pledge, give again that he had robbed, walk in the

How Criminals are Made and Prevented

statutes of life without committing iniquity, he shall surely live." If, mark you, if the wicked restore, for retention is not merely a continuance of the old iniquity, but a new iniquity in itself; and to profess repentance, and yet retain, is a greater sin than the original iniquity, in which there was no pretence of thinking about sin or God. "To confess," says Lord Clarendon again, "so much weakness as to beg and sue for a pardon, and to have so much impudence and folly as not to perform the condition without which the pardon is void and of no effect; to ride upon the same horse to the man from whom it was stolen and desire his release, without so much as offering to restore it, is such a circle of brutish madness that it cannot fall into the mind of man endowed with reason though devoid of religion." Rightly, therefore, does St. Thomas Aquinas describe restitution as necessary to salvation. So the constitution of that strange but interesting body, the American Shakers, enacts that before the reception of a candidate "he who has in any way morally wronged a fellow-creature shall make restitution to the satisfaction of the person injured." And the revivalist Moody said, apropos of Zacchæus: "I would not give much for a

Commercial Morality Tending to Crime

man's conversion if he does not make restitution. Make your friends have confidence in your religion by seeing this. If you have defrauded any, go and confess and make restitution like a man."

Restitution has to be made when in any way a man has wronged his neighbour, and not merely in the consequences of theft or commercial immorality. In things spiritual, when right teaching has not been given, or wrong teaching has been given, to those under our charge or influence. In bodily matters, as when we have caused bodily injury or loss, as the law now renders a landlord liable for damages (such as the payment of the doctor's bill) should any serious illness result from the insanitary conditions in a house or tenement of a rateable value not exceeding £40 a year. Restitution must also be made of things civil, such as good character, honour and respect. The injurious untruth must be unsaid to all to whom it has been uttered, as the law of libel enforces in many cases.

But what is chiefly to our point here is the duty of restitution of things possessive, *i.e.*, of real or personal property. If possible, the whole is to be restored intact. On this principle even

How Criminals are Made and Prevented

Judas and the slothful possessor of the one talent acted. So in Exodus we read: "If a man shall cause a field or vineyard to be eaten . . . of the best of his own field and of the best of his own vineyard shall he make restitution." And the Levitical law is: "If a soul sin, and commit a trespass against the Lord, and lie unto his neighbour in that which was delivered to him to keep, or in fellowship, or in a thing taken away by violence, or hath deceived his neighbour, or have found that which was lost and lieth concerning it, and sweareth falsely . . . then it shall be that he shall restore . . . he shall even restore it in the principal, and shall add the one-fifth part more, and he shall bring a trespass-offering." That is, to make restitution, plus compensation, plus a public penalty.

Baxter, in his explanation of the Decalogue, states well certain objections and exemptions from the laws of total, personal, and immediate restitution, as follows :—

What if a man cannot restore the whole? Let him get the assistance of his friends, or confess and pledge himself to payment when it shall be possible.

Must he confess if his disgrace or ruin is thereby

Commercial Morality Tending to Crime

probable? Few creditors would be so inhuman receivers, but, if they were, *fiat justitia ruat cælum*. (The bearing of the case of Constance Kent on this point will be clear to all.) Practice, however, administering rather equity than the rigour of the law, allows restitution to be made anonymously through others, and probably few clergy worth their salt have not so made restitution on behalf of those they have moved to repentance.

What if restitution will wrong my family? Your family can have no right in what is not your own.

But if the offence be long past? Yet the debt remains. There is no Statute of Limitations with God.

Who are bound to restore? Stewards, guardians, servants, when the injury arose from their negligence, though not through their dishonesty. And if one receives by a *bona-fide* gift, but is morally incapable of receiving (as in the case of a bribe), he is bound to restore either to the giver, the Church, or the State.

Are we bound to restore what our father took or owed? If we have inherited what was wrongfully taken, he can give no right to what was not his own. Sinful keeping is as bad as sinful getting.

How Criminals are Made and Prevented

Am I bound to restore what another took? Yes, if you were to him an Ahithophel by evil counsel, a Rebekah by commanding him to sin, an Eli by not restraining, an Eve by temptation, a Sapphira by sharing in the profits of sin.

And when must I restore? As quickly as possible. No absolution would be given to one who had no firm purpose of restitution, or proposed to do it by will, or when he could make full restitution will only make it by instalments, to the discomfort or against the desire of the injured person.

To whom must we restore? Nearly always to the person from whom the goods have been taken. But the receiver of stolen goods must restore to the real owner, and not to him from whom he got them.

What if the wronged be dead? Give it to his heirs.

But if he has no heirs? Give it to some work of piety or charity.

But if the wronged be unknown? Make very sure he or his representative is unknown, and then give the value or amount in alms by the last rule.

The exemptions from the duty are few, and

Commercial Morality Tending to Crime

chiefly limited to the case of when the creditor or injured person condones the offence or forgives the debt. This remission must, however, be free, voluntary, and not contrary to law, *i.e.*, an income-tax collector could not absolve you from payment of conscience-money for income-tax unpaid on a partially true return. And a composition with creditors, if it be not fraudulent, frees you from the obligation, for composition is a virtual receipt in full. Honour, however, will suggest repayment.

CHAPTER IV

DRINK-CAUSED CRIME

It is a commonplace that much, and even most, crime arises from intemperance, and from time to time some judicial utterance, the estimate of some expert, or the publication of some statistics, brings afresh to our notice this highly unnecessary cause of national loss and expenditure. Judges have placed the drink-caused crime as high as nine-tenths of all crime. Minimizers, influenced, perhaps unconsciously, by their personal use of intoxicants, or still more by their financial interest in the liquor traffic through shares in some brewery company, will often think that only a moiety of crime is really drink-begotten. My own estimate is moderate and based on conclusions arrived at in several ways, and drawn by observers with different points of view, and it is, that half the total amount of crime is due directly, and an additional quarter indirectly, to our drinking habits

Drink-Caused Crime

and the excessive opportunity for their creation, sustentation, and growth.

Commonplaces, however, are commonly forgotten, and it is well from time to time, and with fresh figures and fresh witnesses, to bring the subject to the popular mind. I will, therefore avail myself of figures I obtained as, until recently, Hon. Clerical Secretary for the Temperance Society of the Diocese of Southwark, and will deal first with general police-court charges, and secondly with evidence as to the extent of female intemperance.

I have before me returns made at my request by men above all others qualified by opportunity to note what is the motive power which urges on the daily panorama of misery and shame that unrolls itself in our police-courts. These returns are from the C.E.T.S. police-court missionaries at Woolwich and Greenwich, at the South-Western Court, at Lambeth, and at Southwark, districts which cover just the part of South London in which my work and interest chiefly lay for twenty-two years. They all relate to the first quarter of the year, which is not the worst for intemperance.

Woolwich had 1,015 charges for all offences, and of these 841 were for drunkenness directly,

How Criminals are Made and Prevented

while the missionary adds that "a large number of the remaining cases are due indirectly to drunkenness." Four-fifths of the cases directly drink-caused is a serious matter for the national honour and the national pocket, especially in a place containing a larger amount of persons in constant employment and in their prime than any other. Greenwich, the court coupled to Woolwich, shows a smaller ratio of drink-caused charges, as they number only 917 out of a total of 1,308. Here also the missionary notes that "many also are indirectly through drink." The four-fifths of Woolwich become here but nine-thirteenths.

The South-Western Court, newer and serving a population of a somewhat higher social grade, shows but seven-thirteenths as the proportion of purely and solely drunken cases, the numbers being 786 drunks to 543 "various" offences.

At Lambeth, the missionary took more trouble and gave a more detailed report. Here, the total charges were 1,985, those for drunkenness accounting for 1,109; but, as each case was carefully followed and recorded as drink-caused or not, by the addition of the cases due to drink but not described under that head in the sheet, the number was brought up to no less than 1,736, out

Drink-Caused Crime

of 1,985. In other words, all but 249 out of the 1,985 cases for three months are due to drink. This is well above my usual average of three-quarters. Out of 65 assaults, 57 are put down as partly due to drunkenness, and this will not surprise any reader of police news in a local paper. Of desertions from the Army, 44 are said to be drink-caused, and 24 not. The desertion of the family, however, shows, as any Poor Law worker would expect, a far higher proportion, the figures given being 33 to 1. "Disorderly conduct," again, is frequently but drunkenness with some added offence which brings it into a category considered more serious, and here I find all but 20 out of 142 cases are put down as drink-caused. Going thus from charge to charge, we wonder not that cases with "no relation to drink" are but an eighth of the whole, or, in other words, that intemperance accounted, directly or indirectly, not for my modest three-quarters but for seven-eighths of crime at this court.

Southwark, where one of our oldest and most experienced missionaries was stationed, returned 1,147 cases out of 2,081 as being those under the head of "drunk, and drunk and disorderly." Though not giving such particulars as the Lambeth

How Criminals are Made and Prevented

police-court missionary, he added his conclusion: "More than three-quarters of the charges of disorderly conduct are against persons who admit they were under the influence of drink and whom the police describe as having been drinking. It is also safe to say that three-quarters of the assaults were committed by drunken persons. Half of them were also charged with being drunk, but were not included in the above total of 'drunks.' About one-eighth of the felonies were committed by persons whilst drunk, or by persons known to the court as drunkards." Now, as he gives the total charges under the heads of disorderly conduct, assaults, and felony, we are able to find that to the 1,147 "drunks" we must add at least 291; thus arriving at a total of 1,438 drink-caused cases out of 2,081, or more than seven-tenths.

I think that if these estimates erred at all they were under the mark, and regret that in three of them the proportion of "indirectly caused" was not given as I had intended. But, taking solely the purely drunken cases, we find that riparian South London from Woolwich to Battersea gave in three months a total of 3,797 charges of drunkenness out of 7,718 charges. This might

Drink-Caused Crime

not unnaturally bring the taxpayer to the conclusion that but for intemperance we could do with half of our stipendiaries, courts, and police. When, however, we add the other drink-caused crimes the argument is stronger still, and goes far to justify the remark I once made that London is so orderly and law-abiding that (but for the drink) one police-court with three magistrates might serve for the whole of the Metropolis. This, no doubt, is not strictly accurate, but it indicates what saving of reputation and coin we might effect if only we chose.

The prevalence of intemperance and the extent to which it fills our prisons cannot be left out of sight by any who consider the causes of crime. When interviewed by the late W. T. Stead, an enthusiast whose motives were always right whatever might be thought of some of his words or actions, when I was leaving Clerkenwell Prison on its abolition, I coined the epigram "Crime is condensed beer," and though, like most epigrams, it has its element of exaggeration, yet it contains more truth than many. Some general improvement has been seen since then. Doctors have been converted, first by their patients and next by their professors, and their better knowledge

How Criminals are Made and Prevented

and more scientific advice and practice, have been a great factor in the advance in sobriety in all classes. Public opinion has been enlightened, and even legislation, in spite of the antagonism and the undue Parliamentary influence of the liquor trade, has in several respects checked intemperance and has removed excessive facilities and temptations to the abuse of intoxicants. But, just as with a lessened general death-rate infant mortality has not lessened *pari passu*, female intemperance, which in our fathers' days was comparatively exceptional, has for a long time increased, and socially it matters far more than intemperance amongst men. To take the apprehensions and summonses for drunkenness for the year 1910, there were 140,568 males and 36,497 females in this category, although it is satisfactory to notice that the total of 177,065 is less than the average for the quinquennium, which was 196,273.

The proportion seems much in favour of the women; but the figures which reveal the condition which is most noxious to society are those of the offenders who have been over twenty times convicted. In this class, there are some whose repeated offences have been against property and unconnected, directly at any rate, with their drunkenness;

Drink-Caused Crime

but the great majority are the habitually intemperate. In this class, there were 6,907 men and 5,226 females, so that the happy disproportion between the sexes, evident in the figures for crime generally, disappears. And when we extract the items for the great cities we find that this class of recidivists provided in Liverpool, 661 men, but 1,789 women; in Manchester, 850 men to 1,132 women; in Cardiff, 108 men to 158 women; and in Newcastle, 303 men to 352 women. And as to certain districts of London, there comes to hand as I write a return, issued in July, 1912, by a special committee of the Kensington Borough Council, with Sir Walter Phillimore as chairman. Aware that in the Notting Dale district (known often as "the Potteries," and well known to me when a prison chaplain as a hotbed of intemperance and immorality) intemperance among women had alarmingly increased, they examined closely the matter, and in their report gave the following table showing the number of charges associated with drunkenness :—

Year.	Men.	Women.
1901	206	262
1906	353	425
1911	560	666

How Criminals are Made and Prevented

This tells its own tale, and appropriately ends with the figures known as "the mark of the beast." Here, the overcrowding of the area, and especially the letting of houses out in furnished rooms at practically nightly rents, produced and increased immorality, and in its train came the intemperance which caused trouble and expense to law.

One thing that is often forgotten is that while there is a decrease in the apprehensions for public drunkenness and its *sequelæ*, there may be no such decrease in intemperance. Workers and dwellers in the poorest district too well know how, while men as a whole have become more sober, women have more and more taken to regular and frequent drinking. Also they will testify that many women known to them as habitual drunkards seldom, if ever, fall into the hands of the police. And from a physiological and racial point of view, of course, the constant tippling of the housewife and mother is worse for the home, and especially more productive of harm to the babe, born or unborn, and more disastrous to the family, even when actual drunkenness may rarely be reached, than the occasional drunken bout of the husband. Father's Saturday drunkenness scares the children:

Drink-Caused Crime

mother's daily saturation does not. Well said the Right Hon. John Burns, "The public-house is bad for the man, worse for the woman, and intolerable for the child," and yet what was the case before the Children Act came into being? I think I can most hope to bring the real state of affairs with regard to the drinking by women to the minds and consciences of my readers by detailing what was brought to my notice as Hon. Clerical Secretary of the Southwark Diocesan Temperance Society just before the Children Act excluded children from the drink-shops, and, I believe, has also diminished the number of women who frequent them, or, at any rate, lessened the number of their visits thereto in the course of a day.

One of our experienced temperance workers, a lady with two assistants, hired a room opposite a public-house in Lambeth, and provided it with appliances for speedy and accurate counting. They noted and recorded the number of those who entered during a great part of one day, namely, from 10.30 a.m. to 1 p.m., and from 1.45 p.m. to midnight. During that time—it was a Saturday—into that house there went—

How Criminals are Made and Prevented

Men...	1,182
Women	1,287
Children	107
Babies	111
Total	2,687

What the number would have been if observation had been made for the whole day I cannot say; but it would probably have brought up the number to well over three thousand for a single house in the scandalously over-pubbed poorer parts of Lambeth. Whether also, if the whole day had been taken the women would still have exceeded the men, again I cannot say; but of the four periods into which the watchers divided the day between them the women were in excess in all but one. Thus:

10.30 a.m. to 1 p.m. ...	117 men and 99 women.
1.45 p.m. to 6.30 p.m. ...	294 men and 300 women.
6.30 p.m. to 10 p.m. ...	366 men and 417 women.
10 p.m. to midnight ...	405 men and 471 women.

From some points of view the last line of figures is the most striking and most deplorable.

With regard to the 107 children and 111 babies who followed in their mother's steps, or were borne in protecting arms—save the mark!—it may be said

Drink-Caused Crime

of some that necessary household business took the mothers out and that the children must be with them. But this will hardly be maintained when in the last two hours of a January day there were eleven children and thirty-eight babies exchanging the heated and fetid drink-shop for the foggy and chill night air hours after they should have been in bed. If pneumonia or bronchitis swell the horribly high infantile death-rate, what wonder under such conditions. Of some such deaths, let us not hear the cant of "the Lord taking them"; let us confess the truth that they died because of the mother taking them where and when she did.

These last two hours of drinking are admittedly the most unnecessary and the most harmful. During them occurs the most furious drinking, and from just before closing time on Saturday night comes the greatest proportion of violent assaults, and even of murders, as chief-constables have often pointed out. In fact, there is much to be said for the view that earlier closing on Saturdays is more important to the public "health and weal-th" than Sunday closing. Yet in this instance, typical of what goes on in hundreds of similar places in poor districts, there were sixty-six more women than men there spending the last

How Criminals are Made and Prevented

two hours of the day and week, and they brought with them forty-nine children. Two well-known aspirations occur to me in this connection. That of a once popular song, with which imported brewers' men tried to howl me down at a temperance meeting at Epsom—"Up with the sale of it! Down with a pail of it! Glorious Beer!" And that whispered with shame and sorrow, only partly comforted by a clause in the Children Act, "How long, O Lord, how long?"

But, lest it should be maintained by those financially interested in increasing the sale of intoxicants, or hoped by others that this was a rare and an abnormal case, I had the experiment varied. Saturday, I admit, is an exceptional day—"pay day, drink day, crime day," it is often called in this connection. Therefore, the same enumerators watched the same house on a Friday and on a Monday. The whole day was not taken in either case; but the point we wished to ascertain was whether the preponderance of women drinkers, and the high number of children taken into this house, was observed on days other than a Saturday.

On the Friday, the hours taken were 6.30 p.m. to 12, and in that time there entered 213 men,

Drink-Caused Crime

234 women, 31 children, and 13 babies. On the Monday, in consequence of what had been observed on Saturday, a longer time—10 a.m. to midnight—was taken, and the numbers were 397 men, 424 women, 54 children, and 66 babies, the worst result from the point of view of one who desires the well-being of the home and of the children being afforded in the morning. On Monday morning, one expects the men to be at work, and one cannot but see that the women are largely in the streets, partly shopping and partly pawning. So to 111 men who entered this house between 10 a.m. and 1 p.m., there were 154 women with 31 children and babies.

But it might be maintained that Lambeth was an especially drinking locality. I therefore got a public-house in a poor part of Battersea chosen, the necessary principle of choice being convenience of observation, for obviously a drink-shop with entrances in two streets (as most corner-houses have, and corner-houses are always most desired by "THE Trade,"), or one where passing trams would obscure the view of enumerators, would not be convenient. The selected house was watched on a Saturday at the end of June; but only from 2 p.m. to 11 p.m. Into it, however, in this time

How Criminals are Made and Prevented

there went 1,620 men, 994 women, 70 children, and 40 babies. Here one notices with some satisfaction that the proportion of women is not so bad as was found in the Lambeth instance. For this several causes, local and otherwise, might be assigned; but yet not only do the huge figures tell a sad tale to those who know what they mean to the working-classes, but also when the figures for the last three hours of observation—8 to 11 p.m.—were taken, we found there were 852 men, 648 women, 23 children, and 22 babies. The later the hour, especially on a Saturday, the less the necessity, and even the excuse, for such visits. These are just the hours on a Saturday when domestic duties might be supposed to be engrossing the minds of women, and when children would least be expected to be out of their homes or their beds. Yet this was just the period when the proportion of women to men was highest.

With all possible deductions for lawful refreshment, for defensible expenditure in a luxury that is cheap and handy, who really desires the state of affairs these figures represent? Who maintains that these long hours are inevitable when no drink-shop in Scotland is open after 10 p.m.? Who desires that many women should thus be in more

Drink-Caused Crime

than the danger of acquiring or developing those habits from which their present or future homes, and the possibility of *mens sana in corpore sano* for the rising generation, must in large measure be endangered?

The brewers—not the publicans—tried to bully and scare working men from voting for the last (and best) Licensing Bill by their placard "Your beer will cost you more!" Our beer will in very truth cost us more—in national prosperity and honour—unless we do something more to reduce the ubiquity and superabundance of licensed temptations; to free men, and still more women, from the slavery of inconsiderate habit; and, on the other hand, by the multiplication of opportunities for recreation instead of mere distraction, for healthy interest in the place of artificial excitement, to bring England up to the level of more sane and happy nations.

I cannot pass from the painful contemplation of female intemperance without answering here a question often put to me, What about barmaids? I should say:—

Barmaids are absolutely unnecessary and much to be deprecated. There are certain occupations which it may be needful to employ women in the

How Criminals are Made and Prevented

place of men, but serving in a public-house is not one of them. This is clearly proved by the fact that in other countries, and in our own colonies, not only are barmaids not found, but public sentiment is most strongly against their employment. My friend the Dean of Hereford asked an American who visited him to give his impressions of England. "What strikes you most about London?" he inquired. "Its barmaids," replied the American. "What do you mean? their beauty?" "No," was the quick retort, "Their existence! If you proposed to have women bar-tenders in the city where I live, you would be lynched!" Almost exactly the same opinion was expressed by the Canadian soldiers who came here for the Coronation. They were horrified both at the number of women who frequented public-houses and at the general employment of barmaids. This is sufficient evidence that in other great cities beside those of Britain, and among people of our own kindred and tongue, the employment of women in the bar of public-houses is unknown, and what is disallowed by them cannot be necessary for us. Even here, moreover, there are usually whole districts in which barmaids are practically non-existent, or, if they are to be found, they are the wives or daughters of the

Drink-Caused Crime

licensees, and, as such, they are in a class by themselves, nor have they voluntarily entered the trade from outside. They are generally those who must make the best of a bad job, and certainly they, as I have known them, are the last to desire the conditions of life which their birth or family connections have laid upon them. In South London, for instance, you will find many large houses in which there are no barmaids at all; but the more full a district happens to be of apparently wealthy and idle young men, the more certain it is that a multitude of attractive Hebes will be employed. We cannot be so ignorant of human nature as not to know what is the meaning of barmaids for the West End, and barmen for the East End.

And with regard to the prevailing influence upon many of them of the conditions of their employment and upon its effect upon their future career I would transcribe what I wrote in a previous book on prisons: " A young widow, respectable and a teetotaller, took a situation in a public-house, and was charged with stealing cigars for her sweetheart. She works until 1 a.m. on Saturday nights, and her only Sunday leisure is from 3.30 p.m. to 8.30 p.m. on one Sunday out of three. Are publicans prepared to maintain that they never need or

How Criminals are Made and Prevented

desire to employ people with any religious principles or any wish to practise the duty of public worship?"

"The white slaves of the bar are infinitely worse off as regards hours of labour, unpleasant surroundings, temptation to evil of various kinds, and the impossibility of discharging the duties of their religion, than ever were the negroes whom we freed. And bitter are their complaints, whether they be male or female, of the practical impossibility of their getting into other employment after once they have been in a public-house as servants."

"But for the crowded labour-market publicans would either have to give £10 a week wages, or be contented with servants who had notoriously no character to lose."

Reading this again after the lapse of years, I see no reason, in view of subsequent experience and observation in different ways and from different points of view, to alter what I wrote.

In the same book, in an article on suicide (and I had to study and to report on three hundred cases of attempted suicide for each of my ten years in prison), I find that my conclusion was: "One cannot omit to notice that those engaged in the

Drink-Caused Crime

iquor traffic, and especially the 'prisoners behind the bar,' surrounded by temptation, and forced to labour beyond the hours of any occupation in England, furnish more than their due quota of the number of those who attempt suicide."

With regard to the long hours of labour, two things ought to be noted. First, that it is not the publicans or their employees who desire them; but that the opposition to any proposals for earlier closing, or for Sunday closing, comes from the brewers, whose sole interest is to increase the number of barrels emptied and the amount of trade done in the week. Secondly, that the same iniquity of selfishness is found in the case of the working-classes, who clamour (rightly enough) for shorter hours or even for an eight-hours' day for themselves, and yet are the main cause of long hours being forced upon their brothers and sisters employed in the public-houses. Especially desirable is early closing on Saturday night, both for the sake of the employees and from the consideration that a terrible number of crimes, acts of violence, and even murders, always arise from the late and furious drinking which characterizes Saturday night.

The conditions of labour in public-houses are evil both from the moral and the physical point of view.

How Criminals are Made and Prevented

Bearing in mind that in some cases the daughters of a licence-holder are his barmaids, and that, to my personal knowledge, not a few barmaids are of excellent character and good desires, the language —blasphemous and indecent—which perforce meets their ears every day of their lives is a most repulsive and pernicious thing. Said a publican in South London to me: "Till I came here I would not have believed there were such creatures on God's earth as the women who use this house," and I have known both wives and daughters of publicans who protested that they felt unable to do church work (which I was ready to give them from my knowledge of their own characters) in consequence of the terrible incongruity between their normal environment and the higher work to which I invited them.

The physical evils are not merely the long hours, the temptation to drink, and the free allowance of drink, which is commonly the rule. These, of course, account for many a fall; but the whole atmosphere of the house from cellar to roof is unhealthy in the extreme. It is impregnated with evil odours —assassinating stinks I would rather call them— created by the coarse tobacco smoke, varied drinks, the foul clothes of the poorer customers, and the

Drink-Caused Crime

superabundant gas; while the sour reek which ascends from cellar, bar, and kitchen frequently renders the bedroom even more malodorous than the bar. Phthisis germs are especially multitudinous here, and I have attended in one house two consecutive publicans who died of phthisis on the same bed; and here, as elsewhere, I had occasion to notice what they suffered, as they lay ill, from the ascending air, in which the emanations of all parts of the house blended.

There is, of course, little comparison to be drawn between the barmaid employed in the ordinary licensed house and her sister at a railway refreshment bar. The temptation to drink is the same in either case; but the filthy language of the public-house is almost entirely absent here, and the girls do not suffer the physical harm arising from sleeping in the atmosphere of the house, while the working-hours are also generally shorter.

There is another and very important point to which the attention of careless parents should be drawn. I refer to the iniquity of allowing lads and lasses to enter positions from which they can only emerge with the greatest difficulty. I have not infrequently been asked to get some more healthy and congenial employment for young women and

How Criminals are Made and Prevented

young men who desired to escape from the bar. Usually, I have been well acquainted with them, and have known their characters to be excellent. In three cases at least they were barmaids, and visitors to my own house and friends of my daughters. But when I tried to find a situation, say as nursery governess or companion, for which they were quite fitted, directly it came out that they had been employed in a public-house, no further progress was made. Twice or thrice I have certainly been enabled to get places as under-footmen, or hall servitors in a public school, for young barmen whom I could thoroughly recommend; but here again only with the greatest difficulty could I overcome the disinclination to entertain the case of one who had been in "THE trade."

A caution may be useful to those who accept the yearly statistics issued by Government as giving the truth about what intemperance causes. In a word it may be said that the figures therein contained, though true, give us far less than the truth. I have already shown how much crime is attributable to intemperance, although certain categories do not mention drunkenness. The drunken person commits an assault or wilful damage, and the lesser offence of being drunk and disorderly is not then

Drink-Caused Crime

mentioned or recorded, since it is swallowed up in the greater. People often quote the number of the apprehensions for drunkenness as if this gave the whole truth, whereas they only give the basis from which we begin to reckon. Let me illustrate this in another way. Year after year the "Judicial Statistics" record the verdicts arrived at by coroners' juries. One heading is most fallacious, and the figures given are infinitely below the truth. Thus, of 1,346 cases of "Death by neglect, exposure, or excess," only 699 are ascribed to "excessive drinking"—400 men and 299 women—London claiming but 91 men and 89 women under this head. But in one week I noted three cases near me in South London in which such a verdict would have been more accurate than the one actually recorded. Consider these typical cases—

1. Widow, 75, found by a fellow-lodger lying on the landing asleep as usual.

The Coroner: "As usual?"

Witness: "Yes, since last January I have found her lying on the landing asleep two or three times a week."

The Coroner: "Why did she lie there?"

Witness: "Oh! Drunk, as usual."

She was put to bed, and found there fully dressed

How Criminals are Made and Prevented

and dead next morning. Verdict, because a doctor spoke of apoplexy, "Accidental death!" Surely a sub-heading to this verdict would have been less misleading when Government returns are based on such verdicts—and arguments based on the returns.

2. Woman, 35, living at a common lodging-house, lately sheltered for twelve months in a Roman Catholic Convent in the hope of reforming her from intemperance, "had been drinking in a public-house till past midnight. As a barman was going home he saw a bundle lying in Camberwell New Road, and recognized the deceased." No one saw an accident, but it seemed from her injuries that she must have been run over. "Accidental death"; but such accidents are more probable under such circumstances.

3. Man, 60, lodging-house man, "brought in drunk by two of the other lodgers and put to bed." Found dead in the morning. Deceased was a very hard drinker. Verdict, death from apoplexy. Surely in all these cases "accelerated by excessive drinking" might have been appended to the verdict.

Two other points worth notice arise from these typical, and far from infrequent, cases.

First, it will be noticed that none of these

Drink-Caused Crime

drunken persons were apprehended, and at a moderate estimate only about a tithe of those who are drunk in the streets are taken into custody, whether for their own safety or for that of the public. When, therefore, we have the returns of apprehensions, 156,446 in the year, we have only mounted one step of the stairs which lead to the truth as to the prevalence and extent of intemperance.

Secondly, it is idle to suppose that these persons were sober when they left the licensed house in which they were last drinking up to midnight, or that their faces were not as well known before the bar as that of the barman who at once recognizes a supporter of "THE trade" in the dishevelled corpse he finds in the street as he goes home. Yet, while serving drunken persons is an offence against the law, it is observed year after year that "permitting drunkenness" is, according to the police, a very rare matter. The same page of the "Judicial Statistics" which gives me 156,000 persons apprehended for public drunkenness — ignoring the many times greater number of those who (like the above three cases) escape apprehension, and the others who though drunk are charged only with some more serious offence committed when drunk—gives me

How Criminals are Made and Prevented

but 1,214 cases of permitting drunkenness in the whole of England and Wales. The disproportion is provocative of much thought and wonder. The figures for the Metropolis of cases of drunkenness brought before magistrates were 50,967 ; cases of permitting drunkenness, 121. How and where did the drunkards get drunk without drunkenness being permitted, especially when evidence shows their regular visitation and long stay in certain licensed houses?

CHAPTER V

BETTING AS A CAUSE OF CRIME

WHEN I jotted down in 1905, to form a chapter in Mr. B. Seebohm Rowntree's excellent "Betting and Gambling: A National Evil," my impressions and observations as regards betting (chiefly on horse-races) as one of the causes of various forms of crime, and of the type of character that thinks little of crime and readily commits it on the slightest temptation or provocation, I was at first surprised to see how little mention there was of it in the "Jottings from Jail" I published in 1887, after my decennium in prison had ended. The moral I drew was not that I ignored it amongst the many causes of criminality and crime, nor that I considered it unimportant in comparison with the far more common cause—that is, intemperance; but rather that the evil has been increasing by leaps and bounds since then. Nor, indeed, is there so much as might be expected in my later book,

How Criminals are Made and Prevented

"Prisons and Prisoners," although therein, when enumerating "ten desirable reforms" that stood out clearly in my retrospect, I find the following passage :—

"5. The censorship of the Press in the matter of the publication of unnecessary and corrupting details of divorce proceedings and suicide, and of *betting* lists. Editors cannot be the moral prophets of the age while they keep a sporting prophet and while in bondage to advertisers and the lowest classes of their readers. Some crime is State-caused, much is paper-caused."

Said Lord Newton in the House of Lords, July 12th, 1912, "You have temptation literally staring you in the face in the shape of the daily Press and the halfpenny so-called evening papers which appear in the middle of the day, and are really nothing but racing sheets. The newspapers, whatever may be said, really teach people how to bet, and they make things as easy as possible for people who want to bet." "Crime is condensed beer," had occurred to me as a dictum for which there was far too much justification ; but "Crime is the fruit of betting" neither seemed to me then, nor seems to me now, a tenable adage. And yet how painfully the directness of the path

Betting as a Cause of Crime

from betting to bondage, from Epsom to the Old Bailey, was brought before me each month for those ten years. Before each session of the Central Criminal Court a procession of young postmen for trial, and destined in those days almost inevitably to penal servitude for their first crime, showed how good character, fair education, constant and honourable employment, and sobriety, had all been inoperative against the temptation to steal letters containing money. And why the theft? In almost every case it was that they had been led into betting on horse-races, had lost, and had been pressed for the money by bookmakers under threats of exposure. This was an ever-recurring object-lesson on crime as a product of betting; but the most striking instance I recall was when three chief inspectors of Scotland Yard—bishops in their profession—were charged and sentenced in consequence of their having allowed themselves to be drawn under the influence of some Turf criminals of the most dangerous type. Then, indeed, one thought, If these things are done in the green tree, what shall be done in the dry? If these experienced men of the world, with professional knowledge of the tricks of hangers-on of the Turf, can be drawn into the

How Criminals are Made and Prevented

vortex, what can we expect of the average silly and ill-paid clerk who has some excuse for his feverish desire to add to his inadequate income, though at the expense of others? And telegraph clerks, again, became prisoners through their special temptations. The "straight tip" for which a shilling had been paid, passed through their hands for transmission, and added them gratuitously to the ranks of the *cognoscenti*. Then later in the day, from the same Turf agent came the straighter tip to the smaller circle of artisans and shopmen who had paid half a crown; and later still the straightest tip to the innermost circle of his customers who had paid ten shillings. Not all clerks would have the sense and integrity enough not to think that here was a road to fortune made for them by the expert knowledge of some and the credulity of others. So, too, after Derby Day, amongst the various crimes—pocket-picking, burglary, assaults, embezzlements—that kept dropping in after, and in consequence of, that day, attempts at suicide had their place. The first case that meets my eye in some old prison notes is: "Barman, 22, lost place for giving drink away; lost his savings (£80) at betting on horse-races; therefore 'had the miserables,' and attempted

Betting as a Cause of Crime

suicide." So a London coroner, interviewed on the subject of an epidemic of suicide, said: "I always look for suicides after the Derby. After that event you always find that a certain number of shop-assistants have absconded, and a number of other people have committed suicide. They belong to a class of people—much too numerous nowadays—who want to get money without working for it. They fail, and they then go and jump into the river, or something of that sort. You will always find some suicides after Derby Week." And, it should be remembered, that not only in London, but all over the world, does Derby Day represent the acme of interest and of temptation to many, and produce the maximum of evil *sequelæ*.

And again, it struck me forcibly that betting produced one of the most hopeless types of prisoner with which a chaplain had to deal. The men habitually on the Turf seemed to be the very incarnation of cunning and suspicion and selfishness. They had one prayer and one creed: "Give me this day my brother's daily bread," and "Do everybody, and take care they don't do you."

What I have said will show that I was not, nor could be, ignorant of the existence of the

How Criminals are Made and Prevented

vice as one of the chief causes of crime during the years 1876–1886, when I was daily conversing with prisoners. But, from all I have seen, read, and heard since, and not least from conferences with present-day prison officials, I am convinced that betting has so rapidly and so widely increased of late years that its effects are much more obvious in prison. I had met many sad cases of the ruin of those who were dependent entirely on character for employment, but had lost that character through the embezzlement that betting losses had prompted. But when, in 1902, as one of the Committee appointed by the Rochester Diocesan Conference to investigate the question, I had before me one of our Metropolitan police magistrates, to whose court come almost exclusively the labouring and the shop-tending classes, he made deliberately the very strong statement that, of recent years, he had hardly ever a case of embezzlement to try which was not connected, either directly or *au fond*, with betting. Nor would he admit that this plea of betting was merely an excuse put forward without real justification. On the contrary, careful inquiry into the cases proved conclusively that the plea was a true one. The Lords' Committee were told by Sir A.

Betting as a Cause of Crime

de Rutzen, after twenty-five years' experience of the crime of London, that "more mischief was brought about by betting than by almost any other cause. From personal knowledge, he could say that the evil arising from betting was as deep-seated as it was possible to be. In cases where persons were prosecuted for embezzlement, and betting was mentioned as the cause, he was in the habit of making inquiries, which invariably confirmed their statements." Another Metropolitan magistrate deplored that he entirely concurred with what Sir Albert had said, and added that where the crime had been one of fraud or embezzlement he had invariably found that betting had been at the bottom of it. And to the same Committee Mr. Hawke quoted the evidence given to the House of Lords' Commission to the effect that a large proportion of the embezzlement of the country was due to betting with bookmakers and to professional betting. Here are a few typical cases which came close together in point of time. The first was the notorious one of the quiet bank-clerk Goudie, who embezzled £170,000. He had got into the hands of bookmakers, and they had compelled him to go on by threats of exposure, after the common practice of their kind. The

How Criminals are Made and Prevented

next was that of a labourer's wife, charged with stealing shoes and attempting suicide. She had pledged them to endeavour to recover money lost on horse-races. The police constable seized the poison intended for herself and her children. Her husband was not aware of her betting. The third was that of a caretaker of a chapel near me in Southwark, who had stolen £60 in bank-notes and set up the plea that he had got them at the Alexandra Park and the Epsom Races which he had attended. Next came a clerk who obtained fifteen guineas by a forged telegram. When only seventeen he made the acquaintance of a bookmaker who would continue "business" with him, in spite of his father's remonstrances. The judge commented on the fact that it was this same bookmaker whom he had now cheated and by whom he was prosecuted. He got twelve months' hard labour. The next was a dispenser who embezzled £11 from the doctor who employed him. His downfall was accounted for by betting, and his solicitor offered to give the names of the bookmakers with whom he had been betting, in consequence of whose threats of exposure he had stolen to pay them. Another clerk embezzled £1. In his absence from the office, the manager's sus-

Betting as a Cause of Crime

picions were aroused by a street loafer bringing a betting account for the clerk, showing a large amount owing. He lost fifteen years' good character, and got three months' hard labour. And next came a postman who, in the words of the Recorder, "had been engaged in a systematic robbery of the public service in order to engage in transactions on the Turf." He got six months; but in my time would almost certainly have had five years' penal servitude.

Had one to labour the point, a press-cutting agency would enable one to fill pages with typical cases arising in any week, especially during what is called the flat-racing season, when, as a friend of mine engaged on a London evening paper told me, the circulation was found on inquiry to increase by 50,000 per diem from the time of the Lincoln Handicap.

Bankruptcy, again, may be a misfortune, but is very frequently a social crime, and on this the evidence given before the Lords by Mr. Luke Sharp, Official Receiver in Birmingham, as to betting being a chief cause of bankruptcy is conclusive, and I may remark that I cannot remember the bankruptcy of a trader known personally to me in which either drink or betting, and commonly

How Criminals are Made and Prevented

both conjoined, was not the cause, although either or both of them were often unsuspected until the crash came.

The matter has been made worse in the last decade, and has corrupted a class that had not felt fully the temptation to bet on horses of which they knew, and could know, little, by the plague having spread to football matches. So I wrote once to an editor—

"DEAR SIR,—I am obliged to you for sending me a copy of the *Football Evening News*, containing an article by you, as editor, on betting on football matches, and I am profoundly thankful that it has been written, and that by a person and in a special publication which will cause its straightforward sanity and integrity to come before both the victims of an indefensible absurdity and the blood-sucking parasites who live by the victimization of the unthinking.

"I have seen football healthily grow in favour since the fifties and sixties, in which our school team (of which I was a part) could find hardly any team against which to play, on to the time when it was a part of manly education for thousands as a pastime that taught endurance, promptness of action, and unselfish pursuit of honour.

Betting as a Cause of Crime

But then for tens of thousands it degenerated into a mere spectator's pastime, and a tremendous downward step was taken when it became a vehicle of betting.

"We began first to hear of rows in Australia, because teams had been supposed to have been bribed in the interest of betting to lose—and none are so furious as those who wanted to sharp others and find they have been sharped themselves. Then we heard of shady practices arising from betting on matches in the Midlands and the North, and still we hoped, and hope, that the South of England was free. But the ingenuity of professional betting men has been so great, and the feverish desire to gain unearned money has become so horribly extensive, that, as you say, millions of inducements to gamble in the silliest way are given away to those who frequent football matches. Thus a habit is formed in lads which may vary in form hereafter, but will have left behind a deterioration of character, and an inability for manliness. These "noonday thieves" as you call them—these spoil-sports as they really are—lice on the national head—are apparently, to judge by the Home Secretary's answer to the Football Association, beyond the arm of the law, especially when they confess their real criminality

How Criminals are Made and Prevented

by putting the sea between their offices and those they entice and plunder. But, though laws cannot make men either sober or sane, they can do something to diminish the powers of evil and to protect, even from themselves, those inclined to insanity or insobriety. Laws, however, will neither be made, nor, being made, be operative, unless by the pressure of a right public opinion. All power, therefore, to your elbow and that of the Football Association, in the arousing and sustaining of that public sentiment which shall rescue football from its imminent danger of sinking, as have other sports, into contempt, because the gambler has made them his own."

Since then I have read in the *Birmingham Post*, " Unfortunately, a parasitical growth of a peculiarly harmful nature has fastened on the game of football, and may conceivably rob it of its very life-blood, unless means are speedily found to exercise it." Later, a well-known Birmingham detective said that there were in that city at least twenty agents of foreign betting firms, and that one of them was making a profit of £200 a week out of the hard-earned wages of Birmingham working-men. Then it became necessary to issue an order to the troops

Betting as a Cause of Crime

at Aldershot, in consequence of the great prevalence amongst soldiers of betting on the results of football matches, which order states that "non-commissioned officers have acted as the agents of bookmakers and as intermediaries between them and soldiers." Scotland Yard said that the decks of some of our warships are strewn with bookmakers' circulars, particularly football betting coupons. On three ships at least courts martial were held and punishment inflicted on sailors who had succumbed to such inducements. A bookmaker in our local police-court was fined fifteen guineas for attempting to carry on betting with men on H.M.S. *Inflexible*, and at Bow Street a bookmaker, with £295 in postal orders in his possession, was charged with keeping a house for betting in connection with Flushing football coupons.

Much may be hoped from Lord Newton's Betting Inducements Bill, should it become law, the main provisions of which are set forth in two clauses, the first of which makes it an offence for any one to write, print, publish, or circulate:

"Any advertisement of any betting or tipster's business, whether such business is carried on in the United Kingdom or elsewhere, or who causes

How Criminals are Made and Prevented

or procures any of these things to be done. The punishment for the first offence is a fine not exceeding £25, or three months' imprisonment, and for a second or subsequent offence a fine not exceeding £50, or six months' imprisonment." The second clause defines a betting business as "any business or agency for the making of bets or wagers or for the receipt of any money or valuable thing as the consideration of a bet or wager in connection with any race, fight, game, sport, or exercise," and a tipster's business as "any business or agency carried on solely or mainly for receiving money or any other payment for advice relating to bets or wagers in connection with any race, fight, game, sport, or exercise."

At a recent conference in Manchester upon this Bill Mr. John Lewis, the well-known Association referee, wrote that the Football Association had tried, but without much success, to get the assistance of Government to curtail the football coupon evil. They realized the great danger to the game which this evil constituted, tending as it did to degrade and demoralize people, and he could assure the Conference that all members of the Council of the Association were prepared to do everything in their power to stamp out

Betting as a Cause of Crime

that very dangerous evil. Mr. Wilkinson (Chairman of the Manchester City Football Club) said that one effect of the system was seen in the fact that on three occasions the players of his club had been offered bribes to bring about a certain result in their games. And Mr. J. M. Hogge, M.P., speaking of betting advertisements in sporting newspapers, said that recently in one of the best of these papers there were sixteen columns of such advertisements in one issue, and the revenue from them would not be less than £40 a column. That would afford some idea of the amount of money which was obtained in this way. A close study of these advertisements revealed the fact that they were largely advertisements of people who were preying on the gullibility of the British people. There was one firm in Birmingham which at the present time was advertising under at least twenty different names, and they were inviting people to send sums of 2s. 6d. and upwards for betting tips. All the money went to one office, but different names of horses were sent out in reply. The newspapers which published these advertisements knew that they were fraudulent.

If these parasitic vermin are not resolutely

How Criminals are Made and Prevented

circumvented they will leave not a single head of national sport clean and healthy. Some have been driven out of England, and then out of Holland; but English papers see no shame in inserting their advertisements and making money out of their inducements to folly, to vice, and to ruin. And then these self-same papers pose occasionally as interested in the exposure or repression of immoral practices!

The two last pages of *John Bull* are entirely taken up with inducements to betting and gambling, and eliminating some which relate to racing, we find several firms who have been driven by law first out of England and then out of Holland, and are now domiciled in Switzerland. One describes itself as the World's Premier Football Accountants, and attracts by saying that it has just paid £500 for a bet of 5s., and that over £25,000 was paid away last season. Another firm, likewise expatriated, is "The Oldest-Established Football Accountants in the World." Another is "The Oldest-Established Football Accountant doing Business," and attracts by the proclamation of having paid this season 500 to 1, 300 to 1 (twice), 100 to 1 (five times), etc. A fourth exiled firm of football "accountants" in Geneva is vouched for by

Betting as a Cause of Crime

Lotinga's Weekly and *John Bull* in short recommendations. A fifth is a Turf and Football Accountant, hailing from Glasgow, but finding it desirable to have an office also at Lucerne. And, as I write, I read in a daily paper, "the extent of the evil of gambling on the result of football matches may be gauged from the fact that Mr. C. Dean, the secretary of Clapton Orient, recently received the following note from Portsmouth: "Dear Sir,—I will give you £1,000 if the result on Saturday is Orient one, Notts Forest one." Previously, Mr. Dean received two similar letters.

Now, one can often persuade a lad or man that he knows nothing about horse-racing, and that, therefore, "backing his opinion" is an extremely foolish proceeding; but one cannot persuade them that they are equally ignorant concerning football, for they are not. Therefore this new development of the old evil, this invasion of what should be not merely a sport or pastime, but a healthy recreation much to be promoted in the interests of physical and even of moral well-being, is particularly to be deprecated and combated. Sport after sport, as I have seen, and as the *Birmingham Post* pointed out, has "fallen into disrepute as the direct result of the machinations of the bookmaker," a social

How Criminals are Made and Prevented

parasite who not only sucks blood but poisons it: and then writers in the "sporting" Press have the impudence to describe antagonists of betting as "spoil-sports" and "kill-joys"! Against such mendacious cant one need only quote the words of the by no means Puritan or narrow-minded *Punch* :—

> "At anti-gambling 'spoil-sports' loudly,
>   The 'sportsmen' they would spoil are fretting;
> Good friends, though you protest so proudly,
>   The *true* spoil-sport is—Betting!
>   'Altho' it suits the baser sort,
>   What's sport to them is death to Sport!'"

The writer of the sporting column in the *Daily Mirror* said on December 4th :—

"It is no good being squeamish about the matter. It has to be faced, and the sooner something is done to clear the atmosphere surrounding our national sports and pastimes the better. Well over twenty years ago, when betting was so rampant at athletic and cycling meetings, I was a delegate to the National Cyclists' Union.

"At that time was proceeding one of those perennial squabbles between the N.C.U. and the A.A.A. It was on the question of allowing amateurs and professionals to compete together in cycle

Betting as a Cause of Crime

races, the amateurs to take prizes and the professionals cash.

"The N.C.U. officials were afraid of the A.A.A., although I knew that a lot of them secretly favoured the scheme. I got up and said: 'Why should we worry about the A.A.A. when half of the runners capable of winning off their marks run to the book?' It drew forth a long speech from Dr. E. B. Turner in protest.

"But I was a racing cyclist myself at the time, and I knew what was happening in dressing-rooms."

Betting on the turf is, however, still the chief and most popular form of that which begins in folly and ends in vice, and that it has so terribly increased is owing to the multiplication of "sporting" papers, and to the prostitution of otherwise respectable and useful newspapers by the columns they devote in suggesting to men how to act, by the sporting prophet whom they establish and endow in their paper as a guide to those who want to win the money of others without pretence of giving value in return. Most admit that they could not live if they excluded racing anticipations. Few will refuse the advertisements of the notorious pests who have been driven out of England, and then out of Holland, as harmful to

How Criminals are Made and Prevented

the community. Laws can be evaded by the characteristic ingenuity of vice, but could not be easily or to such a large extent evaded, but for the connivance of the Press. Nay, might we not even say by the connivance of a department of the Government? Mr. Justice Darling, during the prosecution of three Post Office servants for offences connected with the betting system, said: "It appears that any persons desirous of betting have only to avail themselves of the facilities of His Majesty's Post Office, and the officials would take care to provide them with every convenience at a minimum of cost in the way of telephoning or telegraphing, and doing the very thing which the law of the country declares to be to the public disadvantage." With the confirmed gambler little can be done, any more than with the habitual drunkard or the dipsomaniac. Our hope is rather with those who are only just being drawn into the vortex. Even when, owing to omission of right and timely instruction on the part of teachers and parents, there is no sense of the sin of covetousness and the criminality of satisfying the sin at the expense of others, a beginning may be made (*experto crede*) most effectually by pointing out the absurdity of imagining that the office lad or brick-

Betting as a Cause of Crime

layer, the costermonger or the cook, can achieve financial success when men have devoted years to "following the turf" cannot know, and admit they cannot know, by what horse a race will be won. From an adverse review in a sporting magazine of Mr. Seebohm Rowntree's "Betting and Gambling," I quote: "We are inclined, from long experience of racing, to believe firmly that out of every hundred people who bet habitually ninety lose money." "What can you know about the merits of horses you have never seen?" I ask a lad. His only ponderable answer would be, "I know nothing, but I take experts' advice. My halfpenny paper is good and disinterested enough to pay a large salary to some turfman who gives me the result of his exceptional knowledge. I back Augur's 'stars.' I follow Busy Bee." This sounds reasonable, for in these days of specialization we are every day seeking and following the judgment of specialists. But its reasonableness vanishes entirely when one takes the trouble to compare predictions with results. This I have done over and over again, never once with a result satisfactory or complimentary to these *soi-disant* guides of knowledge or even of the probable opinion. This method weans many from a belief that either they, or any expert, can know enough to

How Criminals are Made and Prevented

form a basis for the hope of winning except by the merest and most occasional chance. I had once a correspondence with a professional bookmaker, who admitted that no one could know enough to be a trustworthy guide, but said that he based his "system" on the "starred" choices only of a certain well-known turf prophet. I, however, following his method for awhile, found nine failures in his daily "star" before I came to one that was right, and pursuing this plan for a month found the successes would be few compared with the failures even under these conditions. Why do would-be respectable papers allow their columns to be worse than wasted by such matters, with the knowledge that multitudes catch the gambling fever, not by attending races, but by the attraction of the daily suggestions of these Mahdis of the Turf?

I may add, although facts and figures are here more difficult to produce, that my fourteen years' experience as a Metropolitan Guardian of the Poor, during ten of which I was chairman of a workhouse containing over 1,300 inmates, is that betting now stands only next to intemperance amongst males as a cause of pauperism. The habit cannot be eradicated even in old age and the seclusion of an Infirm Ward, and bets are

Betting as a Cause of Crime

made in surreptitious pence when the larger sums and more frequent opportunities of yore are impossible. The fascination of drunkenness, which is decreasing, is great: that of betting, which is increasing, is greater. The evil effects of intemperance are to some extent confined to the individual; those of the betting habit are rarely so confined.

CHAPTER VI

SAVE THE BABE

PROPERLY to understand the physical causes of the tendency to criminality we must consider the question of the excessive infantile mortality as found in the poorer and most overcrowded parts of our great cities and of our chief industrial centres.

Is it natural for any baby to die? Were it natural, then all or most babies would die, and the human race would dwindle away even to extinction. It is, however, inevitable that many should die under the present conditions of life in cities. Vice, ignorance, unhealthy surroundings, must have a weakening, and even a murderous, effect upon infants. And the matter becomes more serious when we observe how marvellously the general death-rate has been reduced by sanitation, and yet how our infantile death-rate, until the last few years, was practically stationary. And

Save the Babe

still more serious for the nation is it when, with this excessive infantile mortality, we have a steadily decreasing birth-rate. And, once more, the seriousness of the consideration is increased by the knowledge that the decline in the birth-rate is mainly due to what Theodore Roosevelt has described as " the capital sin, the cardinal sin, against the race and against civilization—wilful sterility in marriage." The report of the Registrar General shows that the birth-rate for London was in 1910 the lowest known and only two-thirds of what it was in 1871. Infecundity is a symptom and a cause of a decomposing Society, for empires are built on babies, and it is the child that matters most to the State.

Child-saving work, whether undertaken by the Church or the State or by private individuals, is the chief cause of what diminution of crime we have known, which has caused our prisons to be now emptier, according to the general population, than they have ever been ; and its operations have much to do with the saving or the building up of the child who seems foredoomed to an early death or to a life of feeble vitality, and, by providing a better environment for the early years of life, with the enriching of the State with young

How Criminals are Made and Prevented

citizens of a higher type of mind and of a sounder body, whose babies again shall not so quickly die. The children found in our Homes, Industrial Schools, and Reformatories, our juvenile and our juvenile-adult offenders, being chiefly drawn from great cities and their slums, come from the class in which a far higher mortality and a lower degree of vitality are found than in rural districts. In the bounds of the Rural District Council of Hollingbourne, which includes my present parish, the infantile death-rate last year was sixty-nine per thousand. When I went to Southwark, as Rector of St. Peter's, Walworth, in 1895, I found a death-rate of two hundred and one. But as a Health Authority we set to work on the Council, with the constant inspiration of Dr. Millsom, our Medical Officer of Health, in many ways, and even by the minor aid of parochial baby shows which I instituted, until in my mayoral address I could say, " The infantile death-rate, always a delicate test of the sanitation and morality of a district, and of the presence or absence of good industrial conditions, shows in the last decade a decrease of forty-four per thousand, while the average decrease of London is forty-one. Yet we cannot be satisfied, nor relax any effort, nor grudge

Save the Babe

any necessary expense, while still only Hammersmith, Poplar, Bethnal Green, Bermondsey, and Shoreditch have worse figures. Thank God for general and local amelioration ; but what is natural or non-preventable has not yet been reached, and to create a fool's paradise of complacency is only to provide a playground for knaves." Rural Dorset loses eighty-five babies under a year old out of each thousand. England at large loses one hundred and forty-seven. Parts of London run higher, even up to two hundred, and some of the Lancashire factory towns are worse. Once, preaching for the Church of England Waifs and Strays Society (of which I was for two or three years Clerical Secretary) in a town which calls itself Proud Preston, I asked how they could justify its name when their infantile death-rate was over two hundred and fifty. No Kentish shepherd would retain his place who lost over a quarter of the lambs in his master's flock. The Mayor happened to be in the congregation, was concerned for the honour of his town, and formed a committee of ladies to see what could be done. Enlightened progress in social matters and more recent legislation (including eminently the Notification of Births Act and the

How Criminals are Made and Prevented

Children Act), have made the figures, even of Preston and Burnley, less scandalous now.

These figures, even those for rural parts, include not a few deaths which are not natural in any sense, and are in fact murders, in consequence of parental neglect. Some are accidents? Yes, but, as Dr. Millard, an eminent Medical Officer of Health said at Birmingham, " accidents are nearly always preventable, and too often the word 'accident' is only another way of spelling carelessness." And then he drew attention to what we know too well in our greater cities. There is one dreadful form of "accident" to which infants too often fall victims, especially on a Saturday or Sunday night, and that is what is known as "over-laying." One or both of the parents come home the worse for drink, lose their ordinary sense, and in their alcoholic coma roll over on to their helpless babe and suffocate it. Is this natural death, or a form of infanticide? Unpreventable it cannot be, for infants need not, should not, and in Germany are not, allowed to sleep with adults. If most of such deaths were accidental, then they would be spread over all the days of the week instead of being mostly on those nights when most drink is taken. Also they would be as common in the country as

Save the Babe

in cities, whereas of 1,500 inquests in the year held on suffocated babes, more than half were in London, Liverpool, and Manchester. Happily, the Children Act of 1909 re-affirms the criminality of many such happenings, and enacts that it shall be sufficient to prove that the parent or other adult was at the time "under the influence of drink"—which is a less matter, and more easy to prove, than the state of absolute drunkenness.

And a cognate matter was indicated when a daily paper had an article headed "Astonishing Revelations about Methods of Feeding Children," based on an inquest on a child aged four, done to death by the ignorance of its parents, who gave it not only beer and brandy, and usually "whatever it asked for," and "a double go of what we have," while their moral influence was indicated by the mother's words, "He had such a shocking temper I was bound to give it him." Such revelations, however, fail to astonish those who have intimate knowledge of the utter unfitness of many parents to be parents; of the fact that the greatest proportion of infantile mortality is directly due to sins and crimes of omission, if not of commission, on the part of parents; and that especially the

How Criminals are Made and Prevented

knowledge of how to feed babes and younglings is as foreign to many young mothers as is the power to decipher the hieroglyphics on a mummy case. I myself was not so much astonished at the evidence as I was at the verdict of "Death from natural causes" given by the coroner's jury, and yet in the same month in my own parish of St. Peter's, Walworth, the same verdict was given when experienced medical men deposed that the simultaneous death of two children was due solely to the state of appalling filth in which they were kept. And, not long before, also in my parish, a coroner rebuked a mother for causing the death of her baby by feeding it on oatmeal porridge, saying that "You might just as well have given it brick-bats." "Natural death" again! And a fortnight afterwards there was another inquest on another babe, in the same street, who died from the administration of the same "food"—the same verdict being returned. And as to parental supervision of the food of elder children, a girl in my parish died in consequence of a hearty meal of hokey-pokey (cheap ice-cream from a barrow) and vinegared mussels, typhoid not unnaturally supervening. It will hardly be believed that shortly after her elder brother nearly died of the same

Save the Babe

disease, having only varied the fatal diet of his sister to the extent of substituting cockles for mussels!

I would add that coroners and their juries might well perpend how frequently the inadequate, and even untruthful, terms of their verdicts increase evil by neither painting it in its true colours, nor attempting to deter people from habits or acts injurious to all by stigmatizing evil as evil and crime as crime.

For another cause of infantile mortality and the low vitality of those who survive the first year, or even the first septennium, of life, we must go a generation back, and note the inexperience and ignorance not only of young mothers, but of their own mothers. Would that, if domestic opinion and influence does not exist or is not sufficient, all were prohibited by law from marrying before they are twenty-one, and perhaps also that a certificate of having had some training in domestic economy (including the care of infants) was required of all women before marriage. Why is "the poor little dear weakly"? Because the mothers are immature. But sometimes the folly, and sometimes the sin, of girls (and of their parents in having no control over them—duty

How Criminals are Made and Prevented

and discipline being words largely too old-fashioned to be operative) makes marriages at seventeen not uncommon in the districts I have known best, so that the mother hereafter has only her selfishness and want of prudence or self-control to blame for the state of her skinny, rickety, and often-ailing babe, who, if it lives to grow up, is of little use to the country, and probably soon a burden to it in one way or another.

Again, Dr. Millard says rightly, " Slum property of any kind may be regarded as veritable death-traps to the children who are born and brought up in them." Air that has been breathed over and over again by others, some of them with slum-caused diseased lungs; air polluted by the smoke which Borough Councils will not try to diminish because the factories or works belong to "large ratepayers"; air excluded from sleeping-rooms (which in many cases are also the living and the cooking rooms) at night, though then it is least impure; air contaminated by the dirt and sourness of your neighbour's room in the tenement house, however clean your own may be, is as poisonous, especially to the babe's more delicate lungs with their more rapid respiration, as many things

Save the Babe

labelled poison in a chemist's shop. The latter you need not take unless you choose: the former you cannot escape while you live in an overcrowded area, made worse by the habits of many tenants therein, and by the neglect of absentee landlords.

Another chief cause, operative mainly in factory districts, is that the mother goes out to work, or spends appallingly long hours at some sweated "home industry." And yet the father's drink bill, or, at any rate, the husband's and the wife's together, often comes to more than the wife earns, and therefore, if the "few drops" were dropped, the mother could attend to the home and to the children.

The hope of a nation is in its children, and its chief care should be to guard them from harm, and to give to them all that is best for their bodies, their minds, and their spirits. A child's best friend should be its mother; but when that mother cares little, and knows less, about the right nurture of a child, then the babe has a domestic enemy against which the State has little power to fight. Babes die because they have not been given a fair chance of living by those who are responsible for their life. Well is it, therefore, that the State, especially in the last decade, in fighting against the obstructive fetish

How Criminals are Made and Prevented

of "the liberty of the subject"—to do harm—has passed Acts to protect the child, and even the babe, from its natural protectors, from the shepherds who are worse than wolves, and has by other Acts destroyed even parental rights in certain cases, and given them to guardians or societies more to be trusted.

But here one must append a few words as to the synchronous loss to the State of the babes who do not die because they are not born. Mr. Theodore Roosevelt, in a preface to Mr. O. C. Beale's book on "Racial Decay," a work full of fearful facts and striking statistics, speaks of "the capital sin, the cardinal sin, against the race and against civilization—wilful sterility in marriage," and he concludes, "If the processes now at work for a generation continue to work in the same manner and at the same rate of increase, France will not carry the weight in the civilized world that Belgium now does, nor the English-speaking peoples that of the Spanish-speaking peoples; and the future of the white race will rest in the hands of the German or the Slav."

The Report of the Registrar-General shows that the birth-rate for London was in 1910 the lowest known, and it declares that "the main

Save the Babe

cause is the diminished fertility among married women." That year it was 23 per thousand population, as compared with 24 in 1909, with 25 in 1903, with 26 in 1906, with 27 in 1904, with 28 in 1903, with 31 in 1891, with 34 in 1881, and 35 in 1871. A few papers, notably the *Lancet* and the *Church Times*, have been instant with plain-speaking and earnest warning, recognizing not only the facts, but also that prudery as well as pruriency is responsible for the evil. Forcible warnings were uttered in ancient Rome, but, disregarded, availed not to avert the decline and fall of the empire. Horace's *Vitio parentum rara juventus* describes our condition now. Bossuet saw the beginning of the evil in modern France, and exclaimed, " May those marriages be accursed by God and man in which children are not desired, and whose vows are for sterility!" Infecundity is the symptom and the cause of a decomposing Society. The violation of Nature's laws and the prostration of Nature's ends must always create their own Nemesis, and that not merely in the region of economics, but in that of general morality, for, as Prof. Nitz says, "when pleasure is desired and sought for its own sake, without the responsibility and consequence of having

How Criminals are Made and Prevented

children, matrimony loses its entire purpose, and becomes nothing else than a form of monogamic prostitution." Honour be to fecund marriages: honour to virtuous celibacy: but dishonour to all else. Not a word is to be said against child restriction, when necessary, by conjugal prudence, moral restraint, and self-denial in things lawful, as advocated by Malthus; but nothing is more dishonest than the claim of his authority by Neo-Malthusianism or the Malthusian League. As Professor Flint says, " Malthus would have disowned with horror the Malthusian League," which has advocated and promoted with appalling success child-restriction by genetic frauds, family suicide leading to racial decay. Marriages in the upper and middle classes are now made to be so sterile that quite an undue and dangerous proportion of the rising generation is formed of the lower and more ignorant population. Three crimes are common and increasing—the destruction of the seed, of the unborn, and of the body. They only vary in accident: the criminal motive is the same. The disastrous effects to the race, to morality, and commonly to the health of the woman, are the same. Nor can any one pretend that in teaching the way of child-prevention h(

Save the Babe

or she is not also making seduction easy by depriving it of the salutary fear of consequences. The remedy seems to lie chiefly in the hands of the clergy, the doctors (and chemists), and the Press. The Lambeth Conference of Bishops in 1908, moved largely, I believe, by Colonial Bishops, who knew more of the evil, carried unanimously the resolution that it regarded "with alarm the growing practice of the artificial restriction of the family, and earnestly calls upon all Christian people to discountenance it as demoralizing to character and hostile to national welfare"; that it "affirms that deliberate tampering with nascent life is repugnant to Christian morality"; and that it "expresses most cordial appreciation of the services rendered by those medical men who have borne courageous testimony against such things." Whatever we may hope concerning medical men and chemists in Great Britain, the evidence coming from America and Australia as to the practice of many, and even in some places of the majority, of these men who hold the issues of individual and of racial vigour or decay, life or death, in their hands is calculated to make men almost despair of improvement, unless by the influence of a revised religion and morality the

How Criminals are Made and Prevented

demand for the gratification of selfishness continuously decreases.

But when we have done what we can to safeguard infancy, and the babe has survived and come to school age, fresh needs are discovered on its part, fresh responsibilities on ours. The large and important question of School Clinics is, in the minds of many, a pressing need.

The nation has begun to see that degeneracy, like crime, is to a great extent State-caused by sins of omission, and that children against whom the dread influences of evil heredity and environment are already arrayed must have such attention and aid as the normal child does not require, if it is not to join, and to remain in, the ranks of the moral cripples, the physically unfit, and the utterly useless. So we have had in London and other great cities some detached and sporadic efforts of feeding necessitous children (who must not, however, be hungry in their holidays!); voluntary associations for supplying spectacles; local boot funds; and even, on the part of an Educational Authority, the systematic inspection of hair and the quite unsystematic seeing to the verminous children being cleansed; open-air schools for the weaklings; special schools and special teaching for the mentally

Save the Babe

defective: school-buses for the crippled; and even "tooth-brush" drill in places.

All these, however, will fail of their full effect if, firstly, not supplemented by additional lines of action for other needs, *e.g.*, the systematic inspection of teeth (75 per cent. of children in a South London school requiring the dentist); secondly, by the co-ordination or centralization of the separate efforts and organizations which exist for the benefit of the school child; and thirdly, by permissive Acts becoming compulsory, so that ignorance or carelessness, or the interested and undue worship of money-saving, may not hinder in some boroughs that present expenditure which prevents the costliness of chronic unfitness in the near future.

One point I would illustrate and press, namely, that of the cleansing by the municipality, of children found to be verminous after inspection by the L.C.C. nurses, and when preliminary notices and warnings to parents have been ineffectual. This can be effected in London under two Acts. By the Cleansing of Persons Act, 1897, a sanitary authority *may* provide proper appliances and a station to which children shall be sent for cleansing. Many metropolitan boroughs, however,

How Criminals are Made and Prevented

contracted out of this Act—some councillors thinking that local patriotism is shown by their refusing to admit that any serious evil can exist where they have the honour of being concerned in local self-government; while other boroughs neglected to work the Act adequately, the excuse being urged that the matter fell rather under the duties of the Guardians of the Poor, while the real cause was often the influence of the down-with-the-rates-at-any-cost party. But by the other Act, the L.C.C. General Powers Act, 1907, the London County Council has the power to do the work systematically, thoroughly, and universally; but—again from fear of expense (as at first in the case of feeding necessitous children), though here again expenditure spells saving—is chary of using its power. All it has done, therefore, is that in a few boroughs where proper appliances and places exist, the L.C.C. will pay for work done. It does not do its own work directly, and even through others does little or even nothing in the majority of places. Of course it has been contended from the first that the duty should have been put on the sanitary and not on the educational authority, and then the necessary places and plant would have been forthcoming at disinfecting stations or

Save the Babe

public baths. The Act might well be amended in this respect. Meanwhile, in some boroughs, the L.C.C. sends its school-nurses, discovers the evil, sends usually futile warnings to parents, and, if rare prosecutions ensue, no really effective action follows; while in a neighbouring borough a perfect system may be in action. Thus, being conversant with what was done in the borough of Southwark, where I was on its sanitary and educational committees for seventeen years, I inquired (on behalf of the Diocesan Conference Social Service Committee, whereof I was sometime chairman), of all the medical officers of health for the South London boroughs as to how many children were cleansed in the year, and what consequent steps were taken. All having courteously replied, I found that the number cleansed in that year were: In Southwark, 3,000; in Bermondsey, 1,398; in Camberwell, 1,124; in Battersea, 656; in Woolwich, 195; in Wandsworth, 29; in Deptford, 0; in Lambeth, 0; in Greenwich, 0; and in Lewisham, 0.

This is a striking illustration of the inferiority of permissive laws when action is needful. The word "may" should always be at least suspect in a law. Much legislation for the benefit of the

How Criminals are Made and Prevented

working-classes only became generally beneficial when "shall" was put in the place of "may." How well I can remember when over twenty years ago I drew the attention of the clerk to a Local Board of Health to certain housing horrors and pointed out that the then unamended Act said that "the Board may cause, etc." A pleased and satisfied grin spread over his face—"Yes, it ma-ay!" As regards the cleansing of children, the number who will require attention will, of course, vary according to the population and the conditions of boroughs; but a knowledge of the riparian slums of Deptford and Bermondsey did not explain why much was done in one place and nothing in another, so similar in conditions. And plainly the public was entitled to know, and the L.C.C. should have been required to explain, why the Act was apparently a dead letter in four out of ten boroughs.

Again, where children have been cleansed, it is obviously a waste of time and money to remove objects of entomological interest, exasperating activity, and adhesive companionship from them in the morning, and then send them to gather a fresh supply from their beds at night. But I found that in Southwark, Woolwich, Battersea, and

Save the Babe

Camberwell alone was it the rule that while the children and their clothes were being disinfected their bedding was also collected, disinfected, and sent home, and in bad cases their rooms also fumigated and stripped of wall-paper. In Bermondsey that course was taken only "when children are constantly coming from some particular house"—an answer which emphasizes the terrible neglect that must exist in boroughs where the Act is not applied. Over and over are the same children in evil case; but nothing done that is thorough and efficacious.

Again, as in other matters concerning public health, the issue and distribution of sanitary leaflets had been found to be advantageous. I inquired as to whether any printed advice to parents was sent home by the cleansed children or left by the cleanser of the home. Only in Woolwich was this ever done.

Hitherto, the inquiry revealed only what was done—or left undone—as to one matter that would come under the notice and powers of School Clinics if and where established. But a general question on the subject elicited very various opinions. The view of individualists seems expressed in one answer: "They would pauperize

How Criminals are Made and Prevented

the people and weaken the moral backbone of parents by further relieving them of responsibility for all necessary attention to their children"—a position which, of course, voices also the objection to the abolition of school fees and other matters on which the nation has already made up its mind. One both chuckles and sighs at the phrase "moral backbone" when remembering the multitude of parents whose substitute for that desirable possession is comparable rather to a tube filled with mouldy fluff. And the view of individualists and that of professional interests seem combined in another answer, which said that School Clinics are "undesirable, as the parents should be held responsible for obtaining medical advice." Both these views have, no doubt, to be reckoned with.

On the other hand, other medical officers of health said, "provision must be made at the public expense for the treatment of all children who are unable to pay for it." One said "they follow as a natural corollary to the medical inspection of school children."

The real question, however, is whether the consideration of expense is to be dominant to the prohibition or the curtailment of the work, or

Save the Babe

whether expenditure on such a matter is to be regarded as a lucrative investment on the part of a nation which cannot afford to allow the continuous manufacture of an army of expensive, incapable, and undesirable natives. We have suffered too long from that ignorant extravagance which consists in denying or neglecting to give to the child that care and training at the right time which alone can ensure its becoming not a burden but a valuable asset to the prosperity and reputation of our country. It is mainly the weaklings who become our paupers and our criminals; but crime and pauperism are the expensive consequences of our neglect of the weak children before they become the adult weaklings. Grotesque it seemed to me when certain personages or organizations desired that I should encourage the lads of a slum district to enter the Army or the Navy (as I would they could), while from exactly the same quarters came most of the reluctance to "burden the rates" with expenditure designed to produce the physique which would prevent their usual rejection on physical grounds by recruiting officers. Let me from another point of view impress upon people the need of prophylactic observation and treatment of school children.

How Criminals are Made and Prevented

I take now, not the ordinary children of the elementary school, but the boys in a secondary school of which I was a manager. These were in a way picked boys, their being in this higher school proving that they were sharper than the average, and that they had parents whose first idea had not been to get them away from school and out to some wretched child labour, probably in a "blind alley" occupation, at the earliest legal opportunity. They had many of them gained scholarships, and in appearance and dress were above the average. But when they were medically examined, what was found? As regards special defects (which would have been discovered and remedied long before if School Clinics had been in existence), sixty-one out of the hundred and nineteen had various affections of the nose and throat, such as enlarged tonsils, adenoids, etc.; sixty-two had decayed teeth; the vision of forty-four was defective; and one was partially deaf. Thirteen had a lung affected, and two had such serious affection of the lungs that we had them removed, as possibly or probably infectious to their schoolmates. Two had other slight ailments, and one had ringworm. Six were described as not well nourished, and nineteen as only fairly well

Save the Babe

nourished, while one was pigeon-chested and had slight curvature of the spine.

Bearing in mind that these lads were picked scholars and above the average, one naturally asks: If these things are found in the green tree, what will be found in the dry? What would thorough and sustained inspection reveal as to the condition of younger children in our elementary schools in poor districts? And though these lads are certainly not amongst those who seem degenerates and probable recruits for the army of crime, yet what chance of full vigour have many of them in manhood? What chance even of being of sufficient physique to be accepted in the forces or the police, when more than half of them have defects which would ensure their rejection? The good school reports, the obvious intelligence and industry of these boys, prove their possession of a *mens sana;* but when the inspecting doctor appears the assumption of a *corpus sanum* disappears.

But, whatever may be done in the school for the child to fit it mentally and physically for the stress and the battle of life, the influence and the example of the parents will go far to nullify what has been achieved unless it be a synchronous collaboration for

How Criminals are Made and Prevented

good. Take, for example, the ever present, though happily the not omnipresent, evil of intemperance. At the suggestion—almost at the bidding—of some thousands of medical men, the State ordered that instruction as to the nature and effects of alcohol should be given in all elementary schools; but what of the home teaching in this respect? Ignorance, inveterate habit, sheer carelessness, in many a home attenuates, dissipates, even counteracts and destroys the good which has been imparted, and one has to appeal for the child and to appeal to that love for their children which most possess and all profess. You love your children, we say : you would do anything to save them from danger, whether actual in the present, or probable—even only possible—in the future. You know, and act upon the knowledge, that doing something for their future good often involves your not doing something—your self-denial for their sake. We ask therefore : What have you done, what are you doing, what will you do, to guard them against the possible falling into the misery and sin of intemperance?

Do you say, " There is no fear of any child of mine becoming a drunkard "? Why is there no fear? Fifty thousand people drink themselves to

Save the Babe

death each year in England. Do you suppose any of them had parents who imagined that this would be their child's end?

But you think, perhaps, though you would not say it, "Those parents were probably worse or more careless than I am." Are you sure of that? May not many of them have been quite as wise and good, quite as fond of their children, as you are? Nay, do you not know cases in your own rank or calling, cases, maybe, in your own circle of friends or even relations, in which drunkenness has occurred quite as unexpectedly as it would be in your own children? Surely only carelessness or conceit can make a parent ignore the possible danger to his or her own child. What then are you doing, what will you do, God helping you, to forewarn and to forearm your children against the common danger that is at least possible?

Are they forewarned? Have they been taught, not merely as a school-lesson, what is the sin and misery of intemperance? Have they been warned of the insidious nature of many social customs which encourage drinking? Have they been taught never to laugh at drunkenness or the drunkard, nor to use light and grotesque names

How Criminals are Made and Prevented

for the habit and the sin? Have you introduced them to the special teaching and encouragement a Band of Hope can afford?

Are they forearmed? As one of the chief causes of the most hopeless forms of intemperance is the inheritance of the liking for alcohol, or of an inability to resist its effects, have you sufficiently considered whether you might not deny yourself what seems a pleasant and innocent luxury, in order that if a child of yours should fall it shall not be in any way due to the law of heredity? Even the barest chance of harm to a child should surely outweigh any personal pleasure in what cannot be described as a necessity.

And the other great moulding force is early environment, of which the most potent form is parental example. Can children fail to notice, and usually to follow, the example of their parents? Will your moderation certainly be theirs? Had all the fifty thousand who filled a drunkard's grave last year drunken parents? Following the example of your use, is it certain they never can, with possibly more temptation than you and fewer safeguards, come to the abuse of what they first received from their parents' hands? Again one asks, What is custom or pleasure compared with

Save the Babe

the possibility of danger to one's child? Oh! but moderation is as easy as right! Is it? Would not every drunkard contradict your theory? Each one of them was once as you are now.

Consider also the lambs not of your own fold. The family circle is not intended to be the only circumference of our parental love. Your heart will never be deep unless it is also broad. Think of the children of others, the hundreds overlain each year by drunken mothers, the thousands starved, maimed, forced into heathenism, misery, vice, and crime by intemperate parents. Something may be done to rescue, to teach, to shepherd them, by others, as many special societies and noble individuals show. The children note the example, they listen to the words, of others besides their parents. Have you no gospel for them? Are you content that somebody else should do that necessary something for them? If a thing ought to be done, said Archbishop Whately, give a good reason why you should not do it yourself. How often has not the evil done by a parent been cured by the example and words of a teacher, an employer, or a friend! Some step occurs to you that you might take to diminish the chances of

How Criminals are Made and Prevented

some child becoming a victim to intemperance. It is the least you can do, you say, when sympathy and generosity prompt action and self-denial. Do it : and next you will ask : Shall I only do the least I need or can?

CHAPTER VII

TRANSFORM THE LAD

SAVE the babe. Cure, by care, the child. So far, so good. But our aim should go farther than this, and have as its object not merely *deformata reformare* but *reformata transformare*.

It was an old dream of men who studied the nature of metals that a way might be found to transmute the worthless into the precious, lead into silver or brass into gold. Men who professed to do this were found out—as quacks and cheats. What was really discovered was the apparent impossibility of the process. Now, however, a truer, more humble, and yet more hopeful science, aided by new discoveries as marvellous in themselves as transmutation would have been of old, begins to think again of the possibility of the change.

So, in matters relating to humanity, it was thought for long and by many that certain individuals, even

How Criminals are Made and Prevented

certain classes, were incapable of purification, of elevation, of transformation. Impossible in practice, unnatural in theory, and therefore a waste of time, energy, and money, to bring beauty and value out of the waste products of humanity. "Born damned" were many, the child of the drunkard or the criminal, of the feeble-minded or the degenerate, and they must live and die as such. True, great inventors and merchant-captains had taught us that what had been thrown on the dust-heap need not always be left there, and they had made fortunes by the utilization of waste products. But that not only what was despised and rejected of man, but also man despised and rejected by more fortunate and happy men should, by some process not chemical but intellectual, not mechanical but human, not technical but spiritual, be redeemed from inutility at the best, and from infectious rotting at the worst, seemed above the dreams, or outside the merely sordid desires, of the leaders of action. Long before science clamoured to our fathers about the omnipotence of heredity and environment, and had so studied and demonstrated these great forces as to be in more than danger of forgetting they were not the sole forces affecting at any rate man, people had recognized, and, despairingly or with

Transform the Lad

cold fatalism, acquiesced in their obvious effects as seen in the over-crowded and under-vitalized slum.

First, heredity was thought to be irresistible. Family histories were traced out in America and Germany to show how the sins of the parents (or even of one of them) were visited physically and psychologically on the children, and how, even if it were good, parentage could be rendered futile by the law of atavism, whereby children often resemble their grandparents more than their actual parents. The abyss of hopelessness arising from the sole thought or the isolated proclamation of the law of heredity was well expressed by Horace in his miserable cry as he beheld the degradation of life in imperial Rome—" Our fathers' times, worse than those of our grandsires, have produced us who are worse still, and soon we shall produce a generation the worst of the four."

But the next wave of thought and volume of speech urged the even greater power of environment. This was to create all, to account for all, to excuse all. Circumstances make nature and characteristics. If, then, whole classes are found in evil environment; if they acquiesce in it; still more if they seem to prefer it; how can improvement be expected? What hope for children with such

How Criminals are Made and Prevented

environment to act on what a weak or vicious heredity has already so seriously impaired? Sooner could a leopard change his spots, which are superficial, than these social pariahs their ingrained nature. Blame them you cannot. Punish them you should not, save for the protection of the rest of the community. If only a lethal chamber could be legalized! However, admitting all but the omnipotence and irresistibility of environment, some began at once to point out that while heredity could not be changed, environment could. The more one knew and noted the power and effects of environment, the more one recognized the ameliorating and even remedial effects of an altered environment. Thus environment came not as of necessity, but only as an aggravation of heredity, the two together forming an utterly destructive Juggernaut for the children of the degenerate; but its power, it was seen, connoted the possibility of neutralizing one force by the other.

Furthermore, it was seen that a happy result of the experiment of changing the environment for the better was all the more to be expected when the subject of the experiment had a conscious power of helping the experimenter. "The salvation of man lies in his free-will," expresses

Transform the Lad

a truth somewhat forgotten by those who were so absorbed in the contemplation of the normal ways of heredity and environment that they ignored the fact that not infrequently moral and spiritual miracles happened, lilies sprang up from dunghills, strong were some children of the weak, and resolution was potent for good where only a natural and continuous dissolution in evil was to be expected. This splits the ranks of the merely philosophic, and thus one school pinned all its faith on to man's inherent energy, while another regarded all things as determined by blind fate which moved human beings simply as automata.

But simultaneously, and single-eyed amongst the successive fashions of thought as to the power of forces or the impotence of man, there rose the voice of religion, claiming that, great as was the power of heredity, of environment, and of free-will, and hopeless as was the case of the adult whose free-will was consciously and determinedly fixed on the side of his evil heredity and evil environment, well-nigh hopeless even the common case in which dull acquiescence seemed to have eradicated will-power; yet that there was a fourth force—that of the Grace and the Gifts of God. Not that this would operate unsought and unloved

How Criminals are Made and Prevented

("How would I—but ye would not!"); but that, when both the experimenter and the subject could be influenced, and were, either or both, influenced by this other and Higher Power, the conditions of the battle were changed, and the possibility of transmutation was continuously demonstrated. Then the worship of Heredity and Environment as creators was challenged. They remain as forces; but not as the sole forces. When Free-will and Grace come in, the reign of the purely physical is over.

"Change the Environment" now cries the State even for its own preservation and pecuniary advantage. Let education be compulsory and more educative. Let sanitation work its physical marvels. Let even the young criminal be regarded as not outside the transmuting effects of a new environment, and let Borstal rejoice over Newgate.

And as environment is improved, Free-will develops and is inclined to the right side. Self-respect, healthy ambition, divine discontent with low levels and standards, even the aid of a better physique, all are producing a generation of which an ever-increasing proportion are hopeful in themselves and the object of their country's hope.

But inasmuch as the Fatherhood of the State is

Transform the Lad

ever incomplete without the Motherhood of the Church; as the object of transmutation is not merely to effect a change but to bring about the highest form of change; as a fully right and saving environment will produce not merely better muscles or brains or greater desire for higher wage or station, but also the harmonious development of the whole man, body, mind, and spirit: so the Church exists, especially perhaps for the young, to proclaim and to apply the fourth dynamic influence—that of the Grace of God. If and when the State may need the co-operation of the Church in any of its proposals or operations, it must clearly and firmly say, "These things ye ought to do, and not to leave the others undone." In the name of God it must claim for the child full rights and the full development of all and not merely of some of its powers. It was said by many, "Now abide Heredity, Environment, and Free-will, and the greatest of these is Free-will." This is more true than to proclaim heredity and environment, whether separately or conjoined, as the only considerable force. Better, however, to recognize the truth of "Now abide Environment, Free-will, and Grace, and the greatest of these is Grace." "Do men gather grapes of thorns?" despairingly or tauntingly

How Criminals are Made and Prevented

had asked the worshippers of Heredity. Do men gather Victoria plums off a sloe-tree? No; but let a change of environment—a richer soil and a kindlier atmosphere—be given to the sloe, and the thorns (which are, be it remembered, only undeveloped buds) soon begin to disappear and a change in the character of the tree is evident. Then, next, let a better kind be grafted in, and even the old thorny hedgerow plant bears and wonders at its novel fruit.

While we may have the best intentions as to transmuting unpromising material and a few excellent societies and institutions may exist for that purpose, our schemes "aft gang agley" simply because we cannot obtain or retain the raw human material when in the plastic stage. Some sanguine folk hoped that compulsory education would be a panacea for all social evils. But what is the effect of elementary education when neither secondary education nor private study follows it? Does elementary education decrease crime very noticeably? Does it tend to increase the power and the likelihood to commit certain crimes, while decreasing the probability of those that are passional or brutal? What is the real meaning and value of having been in the sixth standard, and what solid result has thereby been

Transform the Lad

achieved which remains as a permanent possession and a basis for superstructures of greater benefit to the individual and to society? Has the child, when emancipated from compulsory education at the age of thirteen or fourteen, really learned much, or even learned how to learn?

All these, without any consideration of how much or how little moral and religious instruction should concomitantly be imparted, are questions which we often discuss, on which we still more often ponder, especially when by our office or position we retain our interest in the lads and the lasses, the young men and the young women, who have been in our minds and hearts in some school with which we have been connected as teachers or managers or members of care committees. Answers to these questions are sometimes given with a glibness and assurance based on theory or prejudice rather than on the observation of facts. The time when the school net was cast somewhat in vain has passed, yet the migratory habits of the lowest sometimes result in the evasion to a great extent of school attendance in spite of all attendance officers and scheduling forays, and therefore a small, though now very small, percentage may be found who are absolutely illiterate, though born long

How Criminals are Made and Prevented

after the institution of compulsory education. Evasion we can combat perhaps; but the more serious matter remains that what has been learned is so rapidly evanescent; that employers complain that office lads, who are supposed to have mastered fractions and decimals, and revelled in problems, cannot add up a bill. Parish priests, too, discover how slowly and badly names are written, or even spelled, in marriage registers by those who, not many years before, have "passed through all their standards."

And this is especially noticeable with regard to women. Take the average married woman in South London. In her single days very likely she was a bookfolder or factory girl, and consequently never had occasion to write, at all events in the course of business, since she left school. Her young man probably lodged in her parents' house, or lived in the next street, and so she had no love-letters to write. Then she married young, and what does she have to do in the way of writing? The landlord gives the receipt for rent, and her husband is living with her. You find, therefore, that those who could write their names daily in copy-books at the age of seven can only write their names very badly at the age of thirty. Then as to

Transform the Lad

reading. When a young mother comes to be "churched" she finds in the Prayer Book certain responses which she has to make, but usually stumbles over every other word, and sometimes cannot read at all. Girls who leave school as average elementary scholars, often gradually lose the power to understand the printed word. Children certainly go into our public libraries in increasing numbers—I sincerely hope the habit will continue as they grow up—but they go to get books for themselves, practically never to get one "for mother to read." Mother makes the excuse more or less justified, that "she hasn't got time for reading"; but if you watch the way many dawdle and crawl along when they go out to do their shopping; if you notice the lengthy periods they spend in gossiping at their doors, and the time they waste in public-houses when "out shopping," you will not be able to pay so much respect as you may desire to the plea of "no time." The number of working-men, in London at any rate, who really read and take an intelligent interest in anything outside their work and "all the winners" is small, but when one takes the case of their wives it is extremely smaller.

And their spelling! In one school with which I

How Criminals are Made and Prevented

had to do, when a child was absent we sent a paper on which the mother should give the reason. The sempiternal errands, for which there is ample time before, between, or after school hours if only mothers would think or manage, appeared in the form of "To go of anarrand," "Detain on arond," "To get some arrants," "To go for a reant," "To go on an arreind," while other excuses appeared on the paper as "Ceapt by his feather," "Whas kept away beCos he Wos hill," "Very pooly so i keep him A tomb," "BeCars He Whas to late," "To late for Scwol," "20 mints two late," "Sent to mis tomkns cool for his hie is Bad," "I will send my sun next monday if hable," "Hat home be cose he Wos so hill i had to give hin son Meesen," "He as bin the Conse," "He plad the truent," and so on, a prize being perhaps deserved for the maternal missive, "bil is got the beleak," which only to the experienced reader would suggest the gastric inconvenience which had kept the boy at home.

But, perhaps, from a new point of view I considered the matter, when in my mayoralty, I had before me the calendar of offenders for trial at our Quarter Sessions at Newington, in May, 1910. Here were 208 to be tried, of both sexes, their ages running from 15 to 70, the great majority,

Transform the Lad

however, being of an age that makes it certain that they have been under the provisions of compulsory education. Taking the first page at which the calendar opened, I found one prisoner aged 17, two 18, one 22, one 23, and one 70. If the last were described as illiterate, which he was not, one might understand the reason. I took another page. One prisoner was 18, three 21, one 24, one 25, one 27, and the last only 35. Plainly these did not belong to a pre-schoolboardic era. But there is a column in the calendar which tells us what is their educational status or standard. At first I doubted whether the number attached to their standards might not mean something different from that with which one is familiar in elementary schools, but on careful inquiry of prison chaplains and prison schoolmasters I found that all had been tested by the regular school standards. And the result? Fifteen of the 208 had no educational figure after their names, some because they were out on bail, and two because they were foreigners. But of the rest nine were unable to read or write; six were placed in Standard I (*i.e.*, the level of the upper class in an infants' school); forty-three were only in Standard II; seventy in Standard III (which a child of nine usually reaches); forty-seven were in

How Criminals are Made and Prevented

Standard IV; thirteen in Standard V; three in Standard VI; and only two could be classed as in Standard VII. Truly, what they had learned had been evanescent from disuse! Of the nine who were quite illiterate the ages were 24, 33, 34, 43, 49, 54, 55, and again 55; while those who could only be classed with infants in Standard I were 21, 29, 38, 38, 59, and 65. Then come no less than 160 out of the 208 who were in Standards II, III, or IV, although it would almost certainly be discovered, if their history were traced back, that the great majority had left school in higher, even much higher, standards than those in which we then found them. That girls of the poorest classes usually retrograde educationally between school age and womanhood is known. But these under notice are mainly men (actually only 14 of the 208 are females), and even as errand-boys or van-boys a certain amount of writing and of calculation would have been required of them, while the observation of even street-corner and pub-propping life would show that they had still a desire and a power to read the utterances of sporting prophets. Yet this, for them, is the result of all the time and labour and money spent on their education, that they are only, at the average age of thirty, where they probably

Transform the Lad

were at the age of ten or eleven. For most of them education has not been evaded, but for most its effects have been evanescent.

And this mental condition is symptomatic of the steady degradation which in other ways turns the intended lad into the hooligan, and the hooligan into the habitual criminal. No large city, certainly not London, or Manchester, or Liverpool, has been unaware of the hooligan, nor destitute of men who have tried all manner of means to prevent his development or to transform him when developed in evil. Some ten years ago a wave, hardly of thought but more of sentiment or fear, passed over the nation as regards his existence and his noxiousness. England is largely governed by epidemics. Suddenly, no one knows why, the attention of the nation is drawn to some particular subject, the rivalry of our too numerous newspapers makes the same subject to be treated in all of them, and perhaps money is raised and even special legislation achieved. The evil to be remedied, the good to be attained, may have been in the minds and on the hearts of experts for many years, but they had only to wonder at the national deafness to their cries until, almost instantaneously, the nation becomes one huge ear. So with the moment came the new

How Criminals are Made and Prevented

name hooligan, which attracted observation more than that of "rough," or "corner-boy," or "larrikin," or "Apache." No new creation, no fresh importation was he, but the necessary and never-absent product of the social and economic conditions inseparable from overcrowded areas, and allowed to wax worse by neglect on the part of the careless or of those whose financial interests obstruct social reform. Chiefly is he the product of his parentage. His lurid language has not been learned in the schools, but from parental quarrels at home. His deeds of violence are but what we should expect from his early and domestic environment of violent speech. Almost as a baby he has heard, "I'll break every bone in your body, you young devil!" as the expression of maternal annoyance at some trivial fault. Maternal, for fathers are negligible quantities, rarely seen except on Sundays. Schools should not be blamed, as they often are, for sins of omission or commission on the part of poor hooligans, for the irregularity of the habits of the class whence he springs not only make him *rarus literarum cultor et infrequens*, but also the constant shifting of residence or "shooting the moon" cause it to be almost impossible for the school net to enclose such migratory and agile fish.

Transform the Lad

A real class, and a real evil and danger to the community, he and his companions of the juvenile-adult order form. But that he was as numerous ten years ago as when he came under my care in prison between 1876 and 1886 I saw no reason to believe. Rather the contrary. The lateness of my return from meetings and services in all parts of London, especially the poorest, during five years in Woolwich and seventeen in Walworth, leaves on my mind the impression that each decade sees an increase of orderliness in the streets. Yet the class is large enough to require special attention, and that all existing efforts for its deodorization and elevation should be strengthened, and even that additional agencies—such as that provided by the Borstal system—of a counteractive and remedial sort should be established. Not numerous in proportion to the general population, not even to that of restricted areas, he is still less ubiquitous. Certain coverts can be drawn with a certainty of finding foxes of this kind, but not every wood, and still less the ordinary open country. From a street or two in Southwark, in Lambeth, in Whitechapel, in Hoxton, in Marylebone, in Notting Hill, and in Kensal Green may come complaints of his habits as an individual, and still more when he goeth forth in

How Criminals are Made and Prevented

bands. Frequently but from one small street, or from two or three courts and alleys, will come nearly all the cases that give the whole parish a bad name. Our modern Alsatias are small, but as indefensible as the larger criminal sanctuaries of mediæval London. Break up the "rookeries," and in their dispersal many rooks change their plumage. *Divide et impera* is eminently true in this respect, and yet municipal authorities have sometimes, to my knowledge, thought it a politic thing to confine criminality and immorality to a definite area, forgetting that therein and thereby they waxed more noxious, and that the worse was the centre, the larger was the circumference liable to infection. Juvenile crime ten years ago was said to be increasing in every country. This was admitted on the Continent, and perhaps in Australia, and notably in America, but escaped notice here for a variety of reasons. But an increase of juvenile delinquency does not necessarily imply an increase in the special form called hooliganism. The savage element might diminish—is diminishing, but depredation might increase by the advance of civilization and wealth.

The hooligan, be it remembered, does not suddenly become such. His inception must be looked

Transform the Lad

for when children show a reversion to the nomad stage of society and begin to be truants and vagrants, and the worst cases are met by truant schools and industrial schools. If not thus dealt with, a few years find the urchin becoming a young thief while still of school age, committing crimes against property, and here the reformatories come in to prevent a further retrogression or downward step. Let the lad continue unchecked or unaided, and then the critical period between youth and manhood produces the hooligan, the offender against the person, the brute who delights in the infliction of pain as much as he shrinks from the thought of experiencing it himself. What shall then be done with him? Those who have remedies to advocate may be divided into three classes. The theorist disciplinarian who says, " Lick him ! "; the theorist humanitarian who says, " Love him ! "; and the man of experience and reason who says, " Do both ! " Eminently in this case it is true that nothing is so simple as to have but one cause or to be met with but one remedy. Certainly he needs not a solitary act, but a course, of discipline, which some find in reformatories, some of the elder in the Army and Navy, and the Borstal system should be so utilized by magistrates and judges as to contain

How Criminals are Made and Prevented

more and to retain them longer. Compulsory service of some kind (not necessarily in the Services) for the masterless, tradeless, aimless young rough, would in many cases—the sanguine will say in most—effect a marvellous transformation. Without compulsion, and for those who can be persuaded to frequent them regularly, lads' clubs, and especially gymnasia, are invaluable; and I would that as many evening gymnasia, with competent instructors, could be opened by the educational authorities of our cities, as there are already evening schools for the other class who desire mental improvement.

In every lads' club or organization you may note some who have more than a capacity for hooliganism born in them; but a better outlet for their exuberant vitality, new interests for their contracted minds, has made them but larky lads with potentialities of strength and valour and virtue. Never must the hooligan be regarded as incurable while still young. He may become so in riper years; but at present he is rather a distorted, than a mortified limb of the social body. He is as much sinned against as sinning, and eminently his foes have been those of his own household. But when from without he finds pity and prompt disinterested love, he will suspiciously, slowly, but surely, respond,

Transform the Lad

and through opportunities for bodily development and cleanliness will come the capacity and the desire for development in other parts of his being. Shepherd the kids; for time is largely wasted on the goats—the adult professional criminal or tramp. Shepherd the kids even before the lambs, for their need is greater and the result of their being neglected more noxious. Uplift the fallen; but still more, prop those likely to fall. Hooligans may be few, and may be diminishing in number; but the salutary questions are why are there any, and on whom does not the guilt of their creation rest when inadequate attention is paid to horrible conditions of domestic and social life, to the habitual over-crowding and under-feeding, the under-paying and over-renting, in which we allow, and practically even force, many of the poor to live.

Not this year, nor in this generation, will they be improved from off the face of the slum. But when the slum goes, and the pubs. and the street "bookies"; when they cannot evade school so easily nor be without more chances, and even necessities, of secondary and technical education, then they will only be found in the records of an unscientific and inhuman time.

I must add my conviction that in two respects

How Criminals are Made and Prevented

our present law, or its administration, fails to do what it might to prevent or to cure hooliganism.

High among the causes of recidivism and of ultimate incurability is the absence of any system of progressive sentences or longer detention for repeated offences of the same kind, and also the absence of any power to enforce a change of habitation by which an immediate return to the old, vile haunts and vicious associates would be prevented. We deport our undesirable aliens: we should migrate our undesirable natives, and place the scene of their former living "out of bounds." And the knowledge that for repeated offences the penalty would increase each time would most surely lead to less inclination to repeat them. Many a man I have known in old days who abandoned crime after an eighteen months' sentence when he knew that it would be (then, but not necessarily now) penal servitude next time.

And the other desideratum is this. Much as one rejoices over the Borstal system and the Probation of Offenders Act of 1907, they fail to do all they should for the cutting-off of the supplies of habitual crime. Probation officers should not have so many to care for as is often the case. More financial assistance for good cases should be provided by

Transform the Lad

the State. Lads should not be put merely on probation who need restraint and disciplined training. The tendency of some magistrates to give the minimum instead of usually the maximum Borstal training is harmful, for while the Prison Commissioners can reduce a longer time of detention in the case of those who are fitted for it, a committal for a year is of little use to those who come from bad homes and criminal company. "Borstal failures" will be seen in the near future to be largely attributable to judicial failure to give an adequate time for training and transformation. And while juvenile-adult offenders belong largely to the class in which some physical evidence of degeneracy and evil heredity is to be expected, why on earth should physical unfitness disqualify them for this beneficent system? As to this, and the general natural history of the hooligan, let me advise a perusal of the book "Young Gaol-birds," by Mr. C. E. B. Russell, of Manchester.

CHAPTER VIII

SOME USEFUL BOOKS ON CRIME

As I write I look up to some eight shelves in my study filled with books on crime, its phenomena, its causes, and its remedies, ranging in date from " A Charitable Visit to the Prisons, containing suitable and proper Advice or Counsel to those who are Confined there. To which are added : Prayers for the Use of Prisoners," published anonymously in 1709 ; John Howard's epoch-making " State of the Prisons," published in 1777 ; and the contemporaneous essay by the Marquis Beccaria of Milan, ancient but by no means obsolete, ingenious and original without being crotchety or impracticable, and both fearless and humane to an extent that is surprising when one considers the age and the country in which he lived. From these we come down to books published last year. Not only in date do they vary, for they range from the Blue Books—"Judicial Statistics—Crime "—for each of

CHARLES PEACE.

To face p. 234.

Some Useful Books on Crime

the last thirty-five years, dry to some, fascinating to others, down to the captious and untrustworthy productions of discharged prisoners ; from a series of the Calendars of the Old Bailey Sessions to poems written in prison ; from the observations, suggestions, and conclusions of prison governors, chaplains, and doctors to the lucubrations of theorists whose dicta are not so worthy of respect as their intentions. Some of my books describe conditions and laws amended or abolished at the bidding both of justice and of mercy. Some are but ephemeral catch-pennies.

Some erect a heavy superstructure on the weak basis of a simple incident, or the experience of a short imprisonment, or of ex-prisoners' tales too credulously received as truthful and accurate. Some deal only with one class or one age of offenders or probable offenders, some only with one aspect of punishment. But others are such as I should recommend or lend, whether I agree with all of their authors' conclusions or not, to those who wished to study what comes under the head of penology or criminology, and it occurs to me that I might helpfully indicate certain recent books as a group useful to the student, giving such a description or *résumé* of them as would make

How Criminals are Made and Prevented

their purport more clear. For this purpose I select first two works of writers who might be called, not invidiously, external theorists, while the rest are by experts whose life-work has brought them into close and daily contact with the inchoate or the actual criminal.

In the former class I place a book published this year, "Criminal Responsibility and Social Constraint," by R. M. McConnell, Ph.D., which should be read as presenting clearly the views mainly held by the Continental school of penologists which would have us believe that we are automata, and that crime in its amount and character is governed by regular and irresistible laws and will present the same average year after year. Morselli's theory is "collective determinism in demographic phenomena," and Herzen declares that only as much as chance exists in the universal microcosm does free-will exist in the microcosm of man. Dr. McConnell's book might be better named from the heading of its nineteenth chapter, "Arguments for the Complete Irresponsibility of the Criminals." It is a work which shows wide reading and close thought, and those who desire to know the faith, the claims, and the tendency of determinism will find it interesting and useful, however little they

Some Useful Books on Crime

may agree with the author's contemptuous repudiation of free-will in favour of heredity and environment as the sole formative forces. His hope and faith "are in the completeness of determinism. All men are of necessity what they are, and cannot be otherwise; they do of necessity what they do, and cannot act differently." When we read in his pages that "normal man simply cannot do evil because he cannot act contrary to his character which has been made for righteousness," we are inclined to ask, Who then is normal? Like not a few sciolists, he makes the large and unwarranted claim that all worthy of the name of thinkers agree with him. "Science is bound up with the denial of freedom in any and every sense of the word." Again, "Many of the world's greatest scholars and scientists maintain that all the acts of every one are necessitated with the same inevitableness as is a flash of lightning or the falling of a rain-drop." Once more, "the doctrine of free-will has now, among most thinking persons, given place to the more scientific view of determinism." Plato and Aristotle, Kant, Hegel, and Hamilton he throws overboard, and adopts as his master Spinoza, who held the soul to be "an immaterial automaton." The author acutely points out that in defining the

How Criminals are Made and Prevented

objects of punishment the lawyer, the sociologist, the psychologist, the moralist, the priest (whom he makes quite distinct from the moralist in aim) the physician, the eugenist, the policeman, the soldier, the criminal, and the injured person will all define from a different point of view ; but he shows an utter ignorance of the ways and works of religion when he says, " The priest declares that punishment is to expiate for sin, to make atonement to the moral governor of the universe through the sufferings of the guilty sinner." A more silly travesty of fact can hardly be imagined.

Having abolished the existence of conscience and of wilful sin and crime in any one, he must, of course, discard all objects of punishment save that—which may be no punishment at all—of segregation for the protection of society. The determinist calls for (and I agree) indeterminate sentences. At the same time he finds it necessary to defend himself against his friends, the more consistent determinists, who maintain that there is no justice in punishing a man for what he cannot help, and that even segregation under the most pleasant conditions is punishment. The book is a mine of information as to what are the pros and the cons of a much-debated subject, and however

Some Useful Books on Crime

feebly and yet with self-satisfaction he attempts to overthrow his opponents, at any rate he quotes them fairly, and with one of these quotations (Naville, " Le Libre Arbitre ") I conclude : " Without an element of liberty there is no responsibility, and absolutely to deny responsibility is to undermine the foundations of all our moral and social ideas: it means that we should be willing to strike out of the dictionary the words duty, good and bad morals, or at least give these words a wholly different meaning from that which mankind has always given them."

The next book to be read, as representing a type of thought or line of inquiry which has a certain following, is " Education, Personality, and Crime," by Dr. Albert Wilson. It should be read even though it may seem a confused and discursive series of remarks which rarely rise to the level of deductions from clear evidence, together with an insufficient number of instances that are *ad rem*. Somewhat forgetful of the truth that nothing is so simple as to have but one cause, no evil so little complex as to have but one remedy, the second sentence in the Preface warns us to expect partial judgments and inaccurate conclusions. In it, the writer affirms that there is only

How Criminals are Made and Prevented

one way in which the difficulties affecting education, marriage, and crime can be met, and that is by bending to the laws of biology, physiology, and psychology. He shows, incidentally rather than of set purpose, how various and even contradictory are the voices of scientists as to the force and effect of heredity and environment on physique and character, as when Weissman teaches that offspring are directly affected by the environment of the parent, but Beard that the embryo derives nothing thence but nutrition and shelter. Rightly also he refuses to follow Lombroso in the exaggerated importance he attaches to external stigmata as evidence of degeneracy. Whereas Bendedikt thinks nothing of even the greatest symmetry, Lombroso would label as degenerates all whose skulls are dome-shaped, keel-shaped, flat, narrow, broad, high, or low, so that it is difficult to imagine how any of us would not be thus indicated as abnormal. Cranial measurements and capacities are shown to be untrustworthy as means of accurate differentiation, and our author would lead us chiefly to rely on what the microscope can reveal as to the pyramidal cells of the cortex of the brain, and generally on the fore-frontal association area of the brain. He would seem, indeed, almost to lead us

Some Useful Books on Crime

to the conclusion that we must procure and dissect a man's brain before we are able to say whether he should be treated as a criminal or whether the State should allow him to marry. As a matter of theory we might agree that "the greatest boon to the nation would be a Marriage Bureau, scientifically conducted under Government control"; but he sees that this would not cover the desired ground unless supplemented by sterilization as "the wisest, most economical, and most righteous procedure." We do not see, however, on what grounds he declares that the neuters would be "docile and unassuming . . . free from vice, contented, and industrious . . . more happy, more healthy and vigorous than the present average man and woman, and deeply interested in social questions, and even in family life," and so on in an aerial optimism which inquiry in Constantinople might shake. Whether free-will exists seems a matter on which he is doubtful, though perhaps he might not commit himself farther than his statement "to the mental cripple there is no free-will," to which the logical parallel would be "to the physical cripple there is no locomotion," as if what is impaired is necessarily non-existent. His ego is a somewhat impalpable thing "only present

How Criminals are Made and Prevented

during normal consciousness," "disjointed under the action of alcohol," "undefinable by psychologists," entirely disappearing under brain trouble, and then giving way to one or more sub-personalities, of which he reckons ten in the case of one woman whose mental fluctuations he especially and minutely studied. We have often reason to dispute his premises even when agreeing with his conclusions, as when, desiring a more righteous estimate of sin and crime, he maintains that poaching is looked upon as "one of the most flagrant of crimes, while he who ruins a girl in the poorer ranks sins under the protection of the law." How under its protection? He is on surer ground when he illustrates the evil results of consanguineous marriages, even when reckoning down to second and third cousins ; or when he describes alcohol as "one of the most powerful agencies towards race degeneracy," and " wonders how any medical man can sanction or justify the use of alcohol as a regular article of diet." Profoundly interested in remedial agencies for social wrecks, he seems to have studied rescue work almost exclusively in connection with the Salvation Army, although he says, "I have been very fortunate in my acquaintance with Church schools. The

Some Useful Books on Crime

influence of the clergy over the staff and the children has been of that character-moulding kind which could only result in raising the *morale* to a high level." Prison, he says rightly, would be curative if the indeterminate sentence were adopted, followed up by wise supervision. A volume more curious than convincing, it yet has value for those who might not appreciate the importance of the physiological and the psychological point of view in the study of the criminal or the prevention of criminality.

I come now to the other class of books, those written by men who have been in constant touch for long periods with the inmates and the ways of our prisons, with those who are apparently doomed to enter their portals, and those who have recently emerged from them.

"Crime and Criminals," by Sir Robert Anderson, is one of present importance as dealing largely with the question of indeterminate sentences and the detention of those who are proved to be unfit for liberty, which must shortly be dealt with not in the tentative fashion in which we have begun to protect Society from those who mean habitually to prey upon it. I wrote more than twenty years ago, " the need of affording protection to the State

How Criminals are Made and Prevented

is also somewhat forgotten in our ordinary punishments, however much they may punish, deter, and afford opportunity for the application of reformatory agencies. When a man's sentence expires he must be released, even though it may be morally certain that he means at once to resume his habits of crime. He may even boast of his intentions; but out he must go, with as much safety to Society as if all small-pox patients were discharged from hospital so many days after reception, whether cured or not." This point, and the necessary corollary of indeterminate sentences, I ceased not to urge by voice and pen, and now Sir R. Anderson writes: " When, after repeated warnings, a man has proved himself to be a moral leper, an outlaw, a criminal in character and habitual practice, to set him at liberty is quite as stupid and as wicked as it would be to allow a small-pox patient to go at large." This book gives us, in an eminently readable form, the conclusions of one with such official experience as Head of Scotland Yard as falls to the lot of few. That crime is decreasing, both absolutely and relatively to population, we are glad to be assured on the word of one who can weigh, and not merely read, tables of statistics. One important exception, however, he notes. The more serious offences

Some Useful Books on Crime

against property, such as the more skilled forms of burglary and swindling, are not decreasing. His view that such crime was the work of but a few men, criminals by profession and choice, and of exceptional ability who seem fascinated by the excitement of planning and executing some grand *coup*, leads him to the advocacy of indeterminate sentences for such, and the expression of a belief that the adoption of this system would at once cause this small band of the *élite* of crime to alter their mode of life. The methods now adopted with such success to prevent the inception or to check the ravages of disease were at first resisted by some as impracticable and by others as an outrage on liberty, but "the next generation may possibly wonder at the blindness and stupidity which characterize our own day in dealing with crime," and will release the unchanged criminal no more than the scarlet-fever patient with the infective discharge.

At this point he has to face the venerable bogey-phrase, "You can't make men—anything—by Act of Parliament." This, he well says, must mean either that outward restraints will not change men's hearts, or else that they avail nothing to control their actions. In the one sense it is a platitude, in

How Criminals are Made and Prevented

the other it is a transparent fallacy. It was ignorance as well as mercy that brought into being what I largely agree with Sir Robert in calling "the short-sentence craze," under which many suffered imprisonment who might have been discharged but for the thought that the sentence was too short to be harmful, while contrariwise it encouraged the habitual criminal to gamble with the prospects of a sentence lighter than those he had already known. Still greater injury to Society has been done by the additional stupidity of measuring out sentences simply, or even chiefly, by the character of the last offence instead of the general character of the offender. Not what the prisoner did, but what he is, should be the consideration of the sentencing judge. If a man picks my pocket, which contains only a pawn-ticket and a farthing, his intention and his act is the same as if he found therein a purse of sovereigns, and he will be the more likely to pick another pocket from his disappointment over mine. Give the man a long sentence for a paltry offence! shrieks the emotional Press or public. Certainly, if it is proved to be a case of *finis coronat opus*. Shoot the dog when he has only torn your trousers? Certainly, if it is an habitual biter, and has already sampled many

Some Useful Books on Crime

calves, although this time his blind fury or your agility caused the damage to be slight.

He has some curious deductions from observation—*e.g.*, "A burglary epidemic, like one of fever, flourishes in mild weather, and a drop of twenty degrees Fahrenheit will check it . . . professional men, burglars included, do not care to be out at night when the thermometer is getting down to zero." This same reason was given to me in Clerkenwell Prison by one who remarked, "'Taint all 'oney, 'ouse-breaking aint!" He sees the value, and the limitations, of such an epigram as that of Major Griffiths, "Our prison population may be classed in two grand divisions: those who never should have been sent to prison, and those who never ought to be released." Recent attention has been so much directed to the former that the existence of the latter has been dangerously forgotten. Worth citing is an epigram of Sir Robert's own: "When this Empire of ours goes down, statistics and liberty will figure in its epitaph among the causes of its fall." He has incurred, and fears not, the wrath of our "humanity-mongers" who never learn and never forgive; but their opposition is fatal neither to reputation nor to progress.

One would have liked to have found here some

How Criminals are Made and Prevented

advocacy of a progressive system of punishment which could precede the adoption of indeterminate sentences, for it is both futile and harmful in various directions to give the same sentence for repeated offences, whereas a frequent offender would consider his ways the sooner if he knew that a repetition of his offence, whether larceny, or wife-beating, or drunkenness, would always mean a longer term or a heavier fine than that experienced on the last occasion. This principle is embodied in the Margarine Act (and should be in the Food and Drugs Act), and when it was more commonly acted upon, in the case at any rate of offences against property, and eighteen months was usually followed by penal servitude, I have known many who expressed their intention to cease a course which would entail a more serious punishment next time. Once a prisoner grumbled to me at a sentence longer than usual. "What did your father do," I said, when you cheeked him?" "Clouted my ear." "And if you cheeked him again?" "Clouted both ears," said the prisoner, and saw the point of the parable. One would like also some explanation, which he could surely give, as to the rarity of proceedings against the notorious receivers of stolen property and the larger makers and distributers of

Some Useful Books on Crime

false coin. Most are well known to the police, all could be easily found out; but the proportion of charges against these is almost as absurd as that between apprehensions of "drunks" and the charges of permitting drunkenness in public-houses. Sir Robert indeed observes that "if we could abolish the market for stolen property, we should go far to put an end to stealing"; but sufficient energy is hardly shown in that direction. Progress has been made with regard to prison reform on several lines, and that simultaneously; but in the reform of criminal law only one idea at the time seems possible to the law-makers. This book is full of interest and instruction for all intelligent citizens, while for the legislator and the administrator of criminal law it is, in addition, an exhortation to more sane thought and action.

"Known to the Police," by Mr. Thomas Holmes, long and honourably known as a police-court missionary of the Church of England Temperance Society, and now secretary of the Howard Association, is not entirely concerning crime and criminals, but is instructive as written from a different point of view to that of most books on crime. His deductions and axioms are therefore well worth noting—

How Criminals are Made and Prevented

People now drink very much less, he holds, but are more susceptible to the effects of drink.

Weakness, not wickedness, is the great characteristic of the average prisoner.

There is less brutality, less debauchery, less drinking; but more dishonesty.

There is no doubt as to the increase in the number of those who live on the border-land between sanity and insanity.

The increase of female drunkards is great, and the list of those constantly charged has grown considerably.

Of the female drunkards (apprehended), 80 per cent. are prostitutes and 10 per cent. demented old women, always in workhouse or prison, upset by a minimum of drink during their short periods of freedom.

Dishonesty among women seems to be diminishing.

The old oaths are out of use or fashion, but emphasis is given to speech by interlarding it with filthy words and obscene allusions.

Police-courts are now the divorce-courts of the poor.

Many ex-prisoners think it is the duty of the

Some Useful Books on Crime

ommunity to help them, in compensation for imprisonment; that they have a duty of restitution never enters their minds.

Hundreds believe that help given constitutes an absolute claim to continued assistance.

Marriages engineered in police-courts are much to be deprecated.

Errors on the side of leniency may be followed with as disastrous results as those on the side of severity.

When a man and woman are jointly and equally guilty, the man always receives the heavier sentence.

Prison discipline is too short to be effectual, too deadening to be useful, too monotonous to be elevating.

A prisoner's behaviour in court has little to do with his guilt or innocence; on the whole, fear and distress are far more likely to indicate innocence than coolness.

Up to the verge of eternity the fear of being homeless haunts the poor.

The one-room home is the cause of much mental as well as physical evil.

For hooliganism five significant remedies are proposed by Mr. Holmes:

How Criminals are Made and Prevented

1. Fair rents for the poor, and a consequent chance of cleanliness and decency.

2. Municipal playgrounds, and organized competitive games therein.

3. The extension of school life to sixteen.

4. No lads or lasses under twenty to drink in public-houses.

5. A considerable reduction in the legal strength of alcoholic liquors.

I would take together, and equally commend, two books by one author, "Crime and Criminals" and "The Modern Prison Curriculum," which appeared respectively in 1910 and 1911. The writer is Dr. Quinton, late governor and medical officer of H.M. Prison, Holloway. A good many years ago Mr. Havelock Ellis, who was a medical man and a student of criminality, consulted me on several points before issuing his book, "The Criminal." He intimated that he was about to send a paper of inquiries to all prison doctors. "I am afraid you will not be much aided by them or by their answers," I said, having observed the little use they made of their great opportunities for physiological and psychological study. This was in 1889, and later came a letter saying how disappointed he was to find the forecast true. Since then, however, the

Some Useful Books on Crime

science of penology has received much greater attention from prison officials, and probably also governors, chaplains, and doctors are of a higher type than in the old days of county prisons and appointments made largely from personal and local considerations. Dr. Quinton is differentiated from most prison officials by having had recent experience as a doctor-governor, as well as a long career as doctor in at least seven prisons. A spirit of optimism runs through the book, and is by no means the mere complacency of an official with the system he has to administer. This could hardly be, since he has lived through so many and so great changes in rules and administration. His conclusion is the acceptable one that steady progress has been made during the last three decades, not only in the reformation of criminals but also in the reduction of crime, and that even the class of habitual criminals no longer produces so large a proportion of the reckless, the violent, and the incurable as in former years. Numbers do not prove everything, and require to be weighed as well as counted; but still, in comparing 1880 with 1909, we find the daily average of prisoners to have dropped, in spite of the great increase in population, and of the multiplication of new small

How Criminals are Made and Prevented

offences, while those in penal servitude were only 3,000, as compared with 10,000. The amelioration of character found in the newer generation, mainly due to outside influences, but partly also to changes in prison discipline, is shown by the reduction of offences in prison from 17,000 to 3,000 in the case of convicts, and from 52,000 to 35,000 in the case of ordinary prisoners, while corporal punishment (now reserved for serious assaults on warders) has dropped from 177 to 35. It being notorious that bad female prisoners are worse than bad male prisoners, it is especially symptomatic of improvement to find that in the case of female convicts offences have dropped from 1,234 to 42, cases of violence to wardresses or fellow-prisoners from 332 to 3, and that dietary punishment has gone down from 189 to 18. Those who credulously lend an ear to inventive or ignorant promulgation of "prison horrors" would do well to note that prison sickness and mortality has been low and decreasing for very many years, so that, as Dr. Quinton says, "if prisons were judged on their health records only, they would appear to be sanatoria outside of which health proper was unattainable." The mortality in 1909 was 4·8 per thousand, and while there is no infant mortality to swell the general rate, yet

Some Useful Books on Crime

this is quite counterbalanced by the fact that prisoners as a class belong more to the unhealthy classes than do people generally outside. Rightly does he join the chorus of those who have—albeit in vain—long protested against the ineffectiveness and expensiveness of short sentences for repeated offences. Such he desires to be "reserved as a kind of warning treatment for beginners."

The Borstal system of treatment of course finds the greatest favour in his eyes, and this method of reducing crime by cutting off its supplies, which are found mainly in the juvenile-adult age (from 16 to 21 years), he describes with interest and affection. The only point concerning which we may be doubtful is that the "Institution Board," which decides on the promotion of those who are improving and hopeful, is composed of the Governor, the Deputy-Governor, the Chief Warder, the Chaplain, and the Doctor, whereof the first three would all be likely to regard matters chiefly from the point of view of discipline, which is not meant, here and now, to be the fetish it was in the old unreformed and unreforming prison system. Each of the points of view represented by the Governor, the Chaplain, and the Doctor should be represented and have due weight; but the Board

How Criminals are Made and Prevented

at present gives three votes to the first and one each to the two latter. As to the indeterminate sentence for old offenders, he sees that the Act empowering Society thus to protect itself was mangled in its passing, and that a subsequent Home Secretary did not view with favour even the small amount of Preventive Detention that we now have, but thought he condemned it by saying that it was in reality penal servitude. Why not, when it is only applied to those who have already been convicts and have shown themselves after discharge to be determined on a life of crime? The fact is that the influence of sentimentalism has lately been unduly great, and in escaping the old Charybdis of a worship of punition and discipline, we are not unlikely to come to harm on Scylla. "Pampering," says our author, who shows himself thoroughly in accord with all the real improvements of the last thirty years, "is unsound in principle and futile in practice." We are quite in accord with his blaming Press and Stage for ministering to the public appetite for sensations and horrors without regard to the truth of statements printed without being tested, or to their applicability to the present time, and even to our land. The "Hibbert Journal," Mr. Begbie's "Broken

Some Useful Books on Crime

Earthenware," Mr. Galsworthy's drama of "Justice" (styled by Dr. Quinton "a grotesque travesty of prison life and treatment under present-day conditions"), and the ever-popular "Never too Late to Mend," which represents only what did exist more than half a century ago, have much to answer for in misleading the public mind. That punishment should be real, and that real punishment will deter, he shows chiefly in his later book. The State must know and dispense justice as well as mercy, and if of two mothers one boasts that she never whipped the most rebellious child, while the other declares that though she does so on occasion, she always gives chloroform first, Dr. Quinton would applaud neither. Incidentally, he pours quiet scorn and decisive refutation on Mr. Begbie's gullibility and consequent slanderous utterances about prison chaplains in his "Broken Earthenware." Though his own work has been that of a doctor and a governor, he is convinced that "religious and moral influences must always take the first place in any rational scheme for the reformation of criminal character. Those interested in prison matters *ab extra*, and without much knowledge of what is done or is possible, have always a heart. But a backbone and a brain are also

How Criminals are Made and Prevented

required, and this book will aid in their development. Some of the aphorisms in the second book are shrewd and memorable, such as—

Many social reformers seem in search of a punishment which will not punish.

Crime cannot be suppressed by cruelty, and it is equally certain that it cannot be killed by kindness.

The criminal promptly avails himself of all the charitable and benevolent theories that are in vogue to account for his existence, *e.g.*, that his crime is all due to his aunt Polly, who, in her youth, stole a canary.

Preventive measures are much more efficacious and trusty weapons for fighting crime than any means the wit of man has devised for exterminating it.

The worse the criminal, the stronger is his desire for association. (This emphasizes what many felt when a Home-Secretary, at the bidding of sentiment, introduced talking at exercise.)

Every criminal is selfish, and every criminal lacks self-control. If criminal statistics are any test of the moral condition of a country, England at the present stands high; but there is still much to be accomplished, so that we must not adopt a

Some Useful Books on Crime

attitude of complacency any more then we need resort to one of despair.

Then there is "The Criminal and the Community," by Dr. Devon, of H.M. Prison, Glasgow, a book to be read just because the author differs so much from most who have a similar post and experience to his. It is very comprehensive, treating of criminology, of heredity, insanity, and sex in relation to crime; of the principles of punishment; of prison life, and especially of alternatives to imprisonment. His own motto for the book smacks somewhat of self-sufficiency, being the quotation from Job, "Great men are not always wise; neither do the aged understand judgment. Therefore I said, Hearken unto me: I also will show my opinion." Most things are wrong according to him—which makes the book a useful companion to one which is more optimistic than otherwise—yet he gives us little clear suggestion of practicable substitutes, and as all men differ, seems to desire a different treatment for each. He quotes not one of the many others who have written on the past, the present, and the future of penological experiments and aims. Moreover, he writes exclusively from a Scotch point of view, which might easily mislead an English reader,

How Criminals are Made and Prevented

since laws and conditions are not quite the same on both sides of the Cheviots. He is right however, and a prophet for any great city, in ascribing many evils, and the most potent cause of crime, to the overcrowding of areas, of houses, and of rooms. Slums stunt and the stunted steal, and he well points out that heredity counts for little, while environment counts for much, and salvation is to be looked for in the fact that while heredity cannot be changed environment can, so that, as he says, " It is more profitable to lead and help the criminal than to encourage him to curse his grandfather." To study the prisoners, to classify them, and to provide the new and right environment for each, is his panacea. But, after all, it is from an improved public opinion, a more lively and brotherly public conscience, and the more general influence of religion, rather than from fresh laws that an improvement is to be expected; for, as Dr. Devon says, "A man may live a thoroughly vicious life ; he may lie, act dishonestly, be cruel and vindictive—in short, break any or all of the Ten Commandments, and yet keep within the law." All that is being attempted as to probation in lieu of prison, of the enforcement of parental responsibility, and even of the abolition

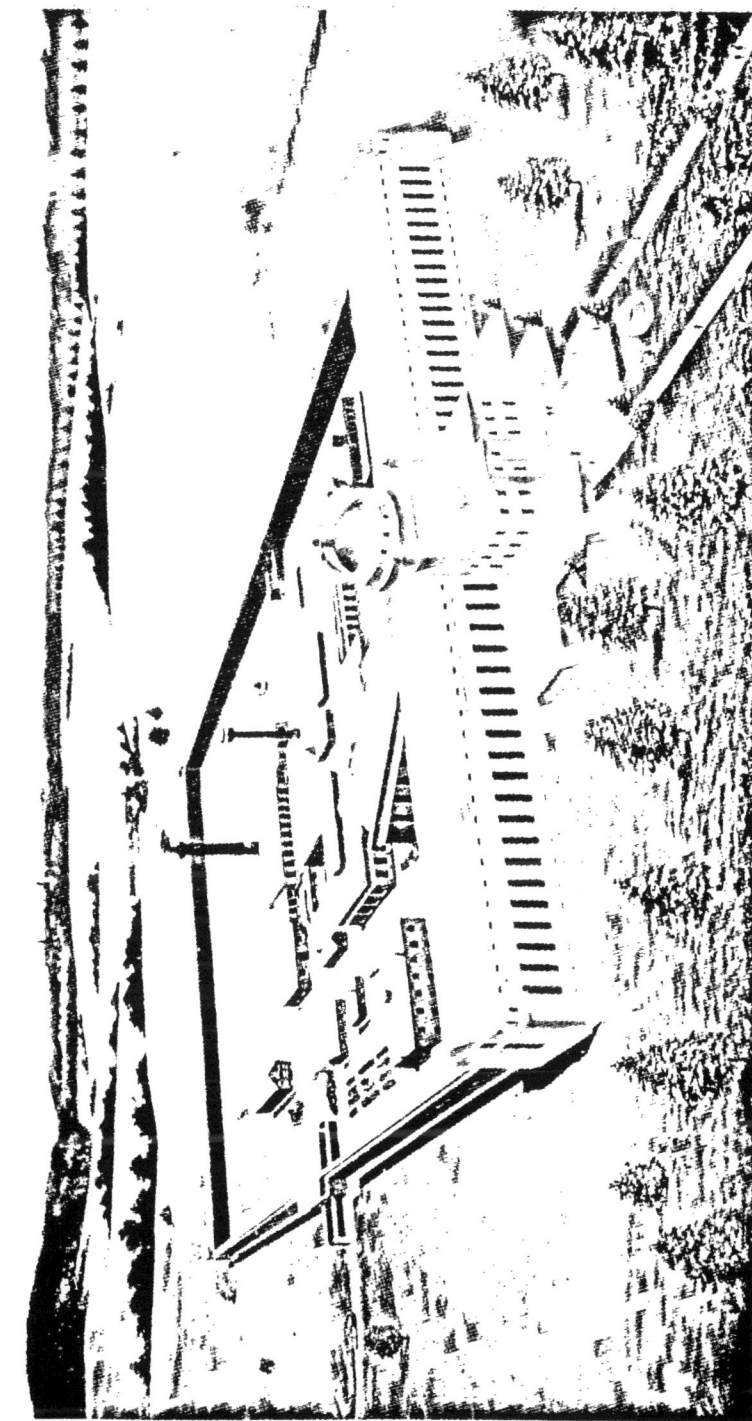

Some Useful Books on Crime

of capital punishment except in cases obviously under the head of premeditated and mercenary murder, has his approval and strong advocacy.

This small library which I suggest to the student would of course be incomplete without a volume dealing specially with juvenile crime and how it may be prevented or treated. Take therefore, " Juvenile Offenders," by the Rev. W. D. Morrison. Though published in 1896, when he was in the prison service, only in detail and as regards recent improvements in law will it be out of date. Penology and criminology are branches of sociology. Our fathers knew not these words; our grandfathers knew not the things they represent, and in our own times England was slow to follow the Continent in these forms of science, Mr. Havelock Ellis and Mr. Morrison (now Rector of Marylebone) being amongst the first to remove this reproach. The first part of the book deals with the conditions, the second with the treatment, of juvenile crime, and the first will be of greater interest to all social and religious workers. The man who takes to crime as a trade, as a rule, begins young. Therefore, preventive efforts with the young should be promoted even more than reformatory measures. Do both; but do the former most. But to deal with the

How Criminals are Made and Prevented

urchin or lad in danger, we must first learn to understand him and the causes which have produced his abnormal state. These conditions are individual and social, and the chief social conditions are parental and economic, or, in other words, heredity and environment. The amelioration of the conditions of life for the young must be our first care. Allow the sties to be dirty, and your little pigs cannot be clean. As I have always maintained, the preaching of "temperance, soberness, and chastity," while we do nothing to remedy or remove the conditions in which these young ones live, is a canting absurdity. That there are fewer children now in prison is no proof of a decrease of juvenile delinquency: it arises from many causes mainly connected with recent child-caring legislation. But where population is concentrated in cities, which again produce more weaklings and more orphans, there will juvenile crime be found. Innate disposition, parental example, the surroundings of the slum, the presence of tempters and of opportunity, are its chief causes, and therefore we must both improve the conditions not only of our cities but of the villages, so that country folk will not be so tempted to rush to towns. Bad landlords, whether of village hovels

Some Useful Books on Crime

with no water, drain, damp-course, or an extra bedroom, as well as of the over-tenanted and over-rented "small property" in the city, are chiefly responsible for crime. It is the sty that fouls the human pig before the pig fouls the sty. Over three-quarters of juvenile offenders are boys, though female complacency may be diminished by remembering that females always get off more lightly than males, that the public and the police are less disposed to charge or to apprehend them, and that their home life and duties shield them from many temptations their brothers meet. Also, be it known that the habit of offending is more deeply seated amongst offending girls than among boys, so that both from industrial schools and reformatories the percentage of failures is greatest in the case of girls. The juvenile inclined to wrong-doing or wrong-life usually passes through three stages, unless checked, shepherded, or rescued in time, and these stages represent a reversion to the early conditions of uncivilized humanity. He first absents himself from any school but that of the street, and is a nomad—a street arab. Then, in contact with Society, he rebels against its laws, preys upon it, and becomes the marauder, the pirate. Then he passes on to insolent contempt for other persons,

How Criminals are Made and Prevented

and delights in hooligan rows and fights. As a Walworth *gamin* would express it: " First you hops the wag, then you nicks, and then you bashes the copper." Truant schools, industrial schools, and the Borstal system, therefore, are designed each to meet the needs of a separate stage of the juvenile's career, and both in amount and in seriousness juvenile crime increases the nearer maturity is reached. Bodies are unhealthy, small, and weak, and the *mens sana* is not to be expected, neither memory, nor intelligence, nor will-power being normal. "Discover and watch especially," says Mr. Morrison, " the illegitimates and the fatherless children, and note that an inquiry in Manchester showed that 68 per cent. of the parents of children in the industrial schools of the county were disreputable, and 14·7 per cent. of doubtful morality." The problem, and the need of child-saving work, becomes the greater when we know the numbers with which we have to deal.

About thirty thousand boys and girls were charged in the Children's Courts during 1910, between four and five thousand are in reformatories, and between fifteen and sixteen thousand in industrial schools, hundreds of the latter being there not for personal offence, but because of the criminality

Some Useful Books on Crime

or immorality of their parents. Yet since the publication of Mr. Morrison's "Juvenile Offenders," the way has been made easier to rescue the child and to cut off the little tributaries to the stream of crime, by the Poor Law Act, 1899, which gave power to Boards of Guardians to "adopt" the children of vicious parents, and even to deny access to them by undesirable relations. Next, the Probation of Offenders Act, 1907, allows delinquent children to be released and put under a shepherd or shepherdess called a Probation Officer, instead of being committed to an industrial school or reformatory, although the deprivation of home and liberty is a known possibility if they do badly while on parole. And, lastly, the variously beneficent Children Act of 1908 codifies previous laws relating to children and introduces valuable safeguards, especially when the parents are intemperate. Mr. Morrison gives us not only statistics as the result of careful inquiry, but teaches us how to inquire and how to construct tables for ourselves, while the animus of the book might be expressed in the words, Seek out and care for the weak and the apparently doomed when they are young : you will do little with them as adults.

There should also be a book in this group

How Criminals are Made and Prevented

teaching us how to study and deal with the psychology of the juvenile-adult offender, and suggesting the inventive, sympathetic, and persevering methods necessary for the reclamation of the young rough whose instincts and the absence of any right influence or timely control have brought him through the nomad to the predatory or even to the brutal type. Such a guide we might find in "Young Gaol-birds," by Mr. C. E. B. Russell, a magnificent Manchester worker for lads and working-lads' clubs. It consists of fourteen sketches of certain young criminals, some irredeemable, some yielding more or less to skilled and elder-brotherly treatment. Each vividly describes a type (for there are no replicas even in the apparent sameness of criminals), and a type the worker, whether in or out of prison, is sure to meet. The criminologist—or social worker—will be interested in certain deductive dicta of the experienced author, such as "the illusion popular among all classes that when a girl has 'got into trouble' marriage will set everything right, is one of the most vicious that can lower esteem for the married life. Such marriages very often make bad worse, and lead to most undesirable forms of domestic infelicity." (But while affiliation is a difficult pro-

Some Useful Books on Crime

cess, and fatherhood often impossible to prove legally, marriage at any rate gives the woman some legal protection in case of desertion.) " Lads need more than anything else an active interest on the part of the older and better men in the workshops." (True, where it may be found; but in how many cases, and in how many ways the corruption of the lad in the factory, or the barracks, or the ship, has come from elders, who not only set the evil example which is more readily copied than a good one, but also actively incite to evil.) " If there is one quality more distinctly lacking than another in the young criminals of the day it is pluck or grit. Taken as a whole, they are a singularly timid, cowardly set of youths." (And, therefore, as he has found, boxing in a well-ordered gymnasium is a blessing to such.) And my experience as a guardian, and as having had a parish at Woolwich containing over a score of fourpenny lodging-houses, makes me entirely agree, as does also my prison experience, to Mr. Russell's observation that " Ex-naval men are very rarely met with in common lodging-houses—affording a strong contrast to their fellows of the sister Service, who form a large proportion of the inmates."

Equipped, then, with these nine books, and

How Criminals are Made and Prevented

getting the current issue of the "Prison Commissioners' Report" and the "Judicial Statistics on Crime," a fairly comprehensive view of crime and criminals, the causes of the one and the remedial measures to be applied to the others, will be possessed by the student or the social worker. Not that these are the only books of the kind, nor that they are all the good ones; but they seemed to me the most interesting and useful group to recommend. Should one desire to study the history of dealing with crime and the improvement in laws, and punishments, and prisons, I should add Sir Edmund Du Cane's "The Punishment and Prevention of Crime," though published in 1885.

CHAPTER IX

ARE WE IMPROVING?

A CHAPTER of generalizations may be permitted, founded on the retrospect of forty years in London spent in and for the prison, the workhouse, and the slum; of work in Shoreditch, Clerkenwell, Woolwich, and Walworth; of the special study and the varied effort involved in membership of the councils and executives of societies for the promotion of Temperance, Purity, and Housing Reform, for antagonism to betting and to commercial immorality, or for the care of the discharged prisoner, the rescue of women, and the provision of homes and healthy life for children who were orphan, destitute, or in peril; and of official responsibility and activity as parish priest in over-crowded districts of the poor, as borough councillor, guardian of the poor, and manager of elementary schools.

Generalizations are of two kinds. Those which are based on isolated or exceptional instances, or

How Criminals are Made and Prevented

from the possession of a dominating theory to which facts must be found or invented to fit and statistics twisted to support : the generalizations of the merely party man or the crank. These are worth little and effect little, except to discredit all generalizations as being deductions from probably insufficient data or a too restricted outlook. Those also, not so easily neglected or controverted, which arise from long observations of multitudinous instances which leave on the mind a conclusion supported by the law of averages and not merely derived from the shock of a few striking examples. If my generalizations are not of the second class it is not from want of opportunity to observe and to classify, nor do I find that they differ much, if at all, from what proceeds from the minds of other observers in the same field of human interest.

My position, on the whole, then is that of an optimist who is thankful for the great results achieved by the action, whether independent or combined, of Church, of State, of Society, and of private Philanthropy during the last generation, and yet sees how accepted principles need further application in details; how salutary laws require sustained vigilance and enthusiasm to prevent evil tendencies or vested interests causing them to

Are We Improving?

become a decrepit if not a dead letter; and how complacency in recent achievement narcotizes those who should be ever watchful against the recrudescence of an evil which has been scotched but not slain, against the rusting of a disused sword, the deterioration of a medicine left on the shelf. My position, in fact, is that of an optimist who when employed as a plumber at the top of a thirty-storied skyscraper in New York, missed his hand-hold and fell, but was heard to say as he passed the tenth floor "All right—so far!" Much has been done to remove wrongs and to give rights: but this is rather a stable platform for further building than a completion of the fabric of social reform.

I would briefly indicate the points as to which I find general improvement, and those in which I consider the present generation to be injuriously affected by evils which are rather variations of what is old than new in themselves. An improvement in general morality as regards its outward manifestation seems to me obvious. It must have been some twenty years ago when I heard a venerable man, Mr. Scott, the City Chamberlain, contrast the sights and the language of the streets at that time with what he remembered when younger, and he found reason to thank God for the great improvement.

How Criminals are Made and Prevented

After those twenty years I take up that parable again. Vice is to be found in the streets, if you search for it and know where to search: but it is not flaunted in our main thoroughfares and outside our railway stations as it used to be. Music-halls are improved out of all knowledge, partly through the pressure of public opinion exercised through the L.C.C., and while the humour of most comic songs is such as to make the lover of literature, or even of sanity, to groan, it is no longer demonstrative or suggestive of foulness. The popularity or profitableness of "problem" plays may be quoted *per contra*; but I would fain believe that dramas born of the idea that the Seventh Commandment was a mistake, and that in holding the mirror up to nature only the dirty part should be reflected, appeal to the decadent mainly, and by no means to the great majority of the nation. Eminently it is not in the theatres in working-class neighbourhoods where cynical and successful immorality on the stage will attract. Again, with regard to obscenity in journals, this has so diminished, that at the present moment one thinks mainly of only one racing paper and of one illustrated dirty rag of the "Bits" type in which the prurient find their delight, while even here the fear of what is actionable is plainly present to the pro-

Are We Improving?

prietors. Even if there are not fewer who delight in such things on bookstalls or in shop windows, it is well known that there are a great many more who not merely object but may be relied upon to take proceedings against the purveyors of moral poison. Papers of the *Town Talk* type used to have some long run for their money: I do not believe they would now live a week.

And, certainly, the common language of the street is another tongue compared with that of thirty years ago. Oaths and obscenity are now the effervescence of drunken quarrels rather than the Homeric epithets of normal speech.

I can well remember, too, when houses of ill-fame were thick in some streets in all boroughs, and the most persistent energy on the part of the Vigilance Society or of individuals (like my friend Canon Jephson in Lambeth) was necessary to induce Borough Councils to take reluctant action. Now, however, neither police nor civil bodies require urging from outside, and other boroughs besides my own are instant in pressing magistrates to imprison brothel-keepers, instead of giving an inadequate and ineffective fine, which used at any rate, to be paid by an association of such folk. "The price of liberty is perpetual vigilance" is

How Criminals are Made and Prevented

eminently and still true in this respect. A change of policy on the part of the L.C.C. or the police, or of any individual Borough Council even, would at once cause the serpents to creep out of their holes.

There has been, undoubtedly, a great improvement in the last thirty years as regards the external manifestation of immorality. Many forms of evil have to be sought that once were brandished in the face of the public, and the efficiency of measures and means, whether for the prevention of evil, the rescue of victims, or the detection and punition of evil-doers, has been widely promoted. What is needed now, it seems to me, is not so much new Acts as the more drastic and uniform application of existing laws, and perhaps a more persistent demand on the part of the public for police action and magisterial strictness. And here we must note the difference between London and the provinces. One city may be ahead of the Metropolis in intelligent and resolute action against immorality and another behind it. A Watch Committee in Manchester may be very different in zeal from that in Liverpool, and citizens have had before now to purge a Watch Committee that misrepresented them in order that a city might be purified.

Are We Improving?

Again, York may have its local Act giving effective power of restraint, while Canterbury may have none, Sheffield may be without by-laws dealing with social evil, while Birmingham may have excellent regulations made by the municipality. The discrepancy between metropolitan and provincial law in the matter of sanitation, and especially housing, is obvious and probably indefensible in some details; and the like may be said with regard to the differences between what can be attempted or achieved against immorality in one part of England compared with another. Nor can it be forgotten that the present activity and thoroughness of police action in the Metropolis is comparatively recent, and I can recall the time when initiative on the part of individuals, of vigilance societies, and of municipal bodies, was by no means welcomed at Scotland Yard.

The chief improvements in law that now might be reasonably demanded are:

1. The declaration that a room in which a prostitute lives, to which she, or he, brings persons home for the purpose of immorality, is a brothel, although no other room in the house be similarly used and although no other person of the same character and occupation lives in the house or

How Criminals are Made and Prevented

tenement. This seems obvious to common sense; but law-courts have decided otherwise. In the Tabard Street area in Southwark, happily condemned during my mayoralty and shortly to be cleared and transformed, our Borough Council could not do what it would because these numerous isolated and single-tenanted dens were not brothels in the eye of court-made law.

2. The difficulty is great of proving ownership, and still more of fulfilling the requirement of the law that prosecutors should prove that such owners "wilfully and knowingly" allowed such use of their property. Much more reform, both sanitary and moral, could be effected if the name and address of the actual owner of each house had to be registered. The devil is not a born fool; and if he was, he has had time to learn and teach his servants many tricks and subterfuges whereby detection can be evaded and law made of no effect; and the concealment of ownership is one.

3. Fines should be made the rare exception and imprisonment the rule for convicted brothel-keepers. In a previous book I urged, with regard to punishment for public drunkenness, that "fines are no real punishment, and certainly no deterrent to the comparatively wealthy offender, and thereby

Are We Improving?

sustain one law for the rich and another for the poor . . . fines might still remain as merciful considerations towards first and infrequent offenders; but their present frequency is a mockery to some offenders and a burden to many that are innocent, yet have to provide the fines for others." Adulterators of milk find a fine a very small deduction from their extra and illicit gains, and I would we would in this respect (and in many others) follow the example of Switzerland, where a fine is only allowed in the first case. In a second, imprisonment follows and the duration of imprisonment depends upon the amount of adulteration found by the analyst. There would be wailing in Wales, if this became London law! But when we come to fines for brothel-keeping, the words "merciful considerations" are out of place, and it is notorious that mutual protection societies or insurance against prosecution renders even a heavy fine of little importance. The profits from the horrible trade are so enormous (as in the case of fines for bookmakers and the keepers of gambling dens) that the monetary loss is but a small percentage off the gains. Too much is left now to the idiosyncrasy of the magistrate who hears the case; but in Southwark we found that when cases

How Criminals are Made and Prevented

of brothel-keeping were taken before a magistrate we knew to be sympathetic, and when our solicitor pressed for imprisonment rather than fine, it became considerably easier to diminish the prevalence of the evil.[1]

Then, as regards intemperance, while the prosperity of the last few years has caused the Drink Bill to go up until it is far more than the receipts of all our railways, while female tippling, and even intemperance, in all ranks of women has increased, and though the House of Lords rejected a Bill which all Temperance Societies (and we have maximizers and minimizers in our ranks) united to uphold, and passed previously one which we had united to oppose ; yet here also a vast improvement is noticeable, and even an increase in the amount spent in drink need not mean a general increase in drinking on the part of the population as a whole, and certainly is not inconsistent with an increase of drunkenness. True, the convictions for drunkenness increased last year, but this represents mainly one class, and, moreover, might be due to greater activity on the part of a police more influenced by a better attitude of magistrates towards the nuisance of public drunkenness, while

[1] Since I wrote the above the White Slave Act has of course made a great difference.

Are We Improving?

this attitude again is influenced by a better public opinion. But doctors have been converted from being (in this respect) negative qualities, or even, in the case of individuals, insidious and successful opponents of temperance, into valiant and vocal advocates of the non-necessity of alcohol to normal beings, and demonstrators of its harmfulness in many hitherto unsuspected ways. The enormous increase and popularity of places of the A B C, J.P., and the Lyons type has revolutionized for good the midday meal of myriads. At public dinners, people are far more anxious to get to their coffee and cigars than to sit over their wine. Again, I can remember when in music-halls the songs were but an accompaniment of the drink, a place for glasses was before each person, and waiters buzzed about with "Give your orders, gents." Now drink is banished from the auditorium, at any rate, of every theatre, music-hall, and cinematograph place, and only a few males find it necessary to leave their seats occasionally "to see a man," *i.e.*, a barman. Therefore, such places are increasingly visited by those who otherwise would have increasingly stayed away as habits improved. Commercial travellers have discovered that business can be done as profitably and less injuriously without drinking. In all Society, if the teetotaller

How Criminals are Made and Prevented

does not take a humorous offensive, at any rate, he is not forced into an unbelieved defensive position. Our young soldiers and sailors and athletes have learned that physical fitness and endurance is contra-indicated by the habitual use of alcohol. Little as Parliament has emancipated itself from the thrall of the liquor interests, yet the passing of the Child Messenger Act, and certain clauses of the Children Act, have shown that it recognizes the truth of the dictum of John Burns: "The public-house is bad for the man, worse for the woman, and intolerable for the child." When I was first interested in Temperance Reform, there was but one of our bishops who was a total abstainer; he was in British Columbia: now there is not one who does not actively support his Diocesan Temperance Society, and probably thirty of our bishops in England are convinced and militant teetotallers. And with an especial significance one has seen that while working men still measure too much their time and their happiness by the "half-pint," yet when they desire a cool head and a steady character to work for them or to represent them as official of a trades union, or on any board or council up to the House of Commons itself,

Are We Improving?

they nearly always choose one who is a total abstainer.

Then, as regards sanitation and housing reform. When an undergraduate at Oxford, I spent part of a long vacation as a volunteer nurse in a cholera hospital in Whitechapel. I was glad of the experience then; but since I have been more than grateful for the cholera. Why? Because of the wholesome fear it excited, which became the direct parent of sanitary and housing reform as embodied in Acts of Parliament. Since then my ways and duties have caused me to have much to do with the study and the enforcement of these Acts, and to write year after year as to the mortality, whether general, infantile, or zymotic, of South London. One began by sighing after the seventeen per thousand, which Dr. Farr considered the line of preventable mortality; one ended (if an end has come) by seeing even London as a whole having a better figure than that. One has come to see the discrediting of heredity as a chief cause of degradation, ill-health, or premature mortality; but also to observe attention increasingly drawn to overcrowding, to tippling far short of drunkenness, and to dirt and dampness, as accounting for evils, physical and moral, which were considered inevitable and still

How Criminals are Made and Prevented

never need exist to anything like their present extent. I will not, however, review what has been done in the last generation, nor recount the aims and victories of successive Housing and Health Acts; nor will I labour the point so well expressed by H.R.H. the Duke of Connaught, "If we wish to keep our countrymen strong and moral, we must think of their houses." And that this refers not merely to homes which are plainly insanitary, whether in the town slum or the village cottage, but also to unnecessary meanness and ugliness of architecture, we are reminded by the words of John Burns, "The people of our poorer towns" (or the poorer quarters of all towns) "suffer not only from lack of means, they suffer from poverty of spirit; their dismal temper is often caused by their squalid environment"; or again, "Spoiled lives in the soiled homes, in the slatternly streets, are often causes of dirt, drink, degradation, loafing, and dependence." And again, "So long as casual labour broods in squalid lairs, in sunless streets, and ugly dwellings are its only habitation, we shall continue to turn out nervous mannikins instead of enduring men." One need go no further than my late Borough of Southwark to see, on the one hand, the awful courts and alleys in the

Are We Improving?

Borough and such irredeemable structures as Queen's Buildings, and on the other, what the Ecclesiastical Commissioners effected in my own parish by clearing away some thirty-three acres of slums and substituting comely dwellings in broad streets, giving an acre of recreation ground, and abolishing obviously superfluous public-houses; or what the L.C.C. is about to do in the even worse slum of the Tabard Street area; or what the Borough Council has done in the provision of some more open spaces, and in the promotion of both health and beauty by the planting of nearly two thousand trees in our streets. These things had a share in our death-rate dropping from 21·5 to 16·7 per thousand. But I would point to the immediate improvement and the far-reaching effects to be anticipated as a consequence of the Housing and Town Planning Act, of 1909. Every county council must now have a "whole-time" Medical Officer of Health. The noxious "may" has been routed by the salutary "shall." When areas are so large and the disinclination to put wealthy house-owning patients to expense may be so great, a County Medical Officer of Health with a private practice should never have been allowed—and would that such were not found still in some

How Criminals are Made and Prevented

boroughs and rural districts. County councils also must (not may) appoint a special Public Health and Housing Committee. The Local Government Board can require special reports as to the sanitary condition of a county or an area, and the particulars to be given are what the Local Government Board wants to know and not what the Council may, or may not, want to give. To close or to demolish a den was difficult, as I used to find. You had to convince not only the local authority, but also a magistrate, and then there was the delay and uncertainty of an appeal to Quarter-Sessions; whereas now the sanitary authority makes the order, and the appeal lies to the Local Government Board. By this Act the building of back-to-back houses, through which life-giving air could never come, is prohibited. Illegal in London, I have seen street upon street of this type built in Leeds and elsewhere. A jury at Sheffield on November 15, 1912, inquired into the deaths of a man, his wife, his son, and his mother-in-law, killed in a fire—returned a verdict of accidental death in each case, and added a rider condemning back-to-back houses. "Everything possible was done," commented Superintendent Frost, the Sheffield fire chief, "but no power on earth could

Are We Improving?

have saved these four people. They had no earthly chance of escape. These back-to-back buildings are the most dangerous class existing, and a similar calamity might happen in hundreds of cases." Inquiries made lately showed that there are over 100,000 back-to-back houses, many of them erected as recently as two years ago, in the West Riding. Sheffield alone has 16,000, although the Sheffield municipality was the first municipality to prohibit the erection of this type of house, and no "back-to-back" house has been erected in Sheffield since 1864. Mr. J. W. Crowther, a member of the Sheffield City Council, affirms that the death-rate is always higher among the occupants of these houses, and that in some parts of Yorkshire, sixty of them were cramped into an area of an acre.

Cellar-dwellings are also now entirely prohibited. Law, hitherto, safeguarded but the poorest, since houses were let with an implied certificate of being fit for habitation only when the rent did not exceed £20 in London, and £8 in the country. These rentals are now doubled, so that the artisan and the clerk, as well as the labourer, are protected. Should there still be a dilatory or faineant local authority, any four inhabitant householders can now

How Criminals are Made and Prevented

set the central authority in action. In not a few under-housed places "perchance there may be four righteous men." Another salutary and radical change is made thus. Rotten dens in slum areas were, and still are, paid for as if newly-built houses. But now if the land is increased in value by demolition under a town-planning scheme (as well it may be) the local authority can recover from the owner a proportion of that increased value. Enlarged powers of entry are given to sanitary officials, and houses are to be "kept fit," otherwise the local authority can do the work and recover the cost from the owner. Mention these points of the new Act in a meeting, even if it be a diocesan conference (*experto crede*), and you will soon hear the whinnying of the "galled jade" and find out who has "a little house property." Sanitary reformers a generation ago had to fight with muskets against an entrenched enemy: now the entrenchments have been blasted and the soldiers have arms of precision in their hands.

As regards prison reform I have already in my "Jottings from Jail" (1887), my "Prisons and Prisoners" (1898) and my "I Remember" (1911) indicated and expressed gratitude for continued progress in this respect, although in my Annual

Are We Improving?

Report to the Prison Commissioners for 1883 I ventured to say, "As a diligent reader and student of all that relates to prisons in all countries and times, while deeply thankful for the progress in prison reform made in the last half-century, I yet see danger in the very perfection in most matters which has been attained. That danger is in the non-development of the moral element *pari passu* with the improvement in sanitation and discipline. The system is becoming mechanical: discipline is almost everything; and the aspect of the reformation of the offender is in danger of being forgotten." And in my next I said: "I am not proud of England when I find what special efforts are made in America and Canada for the reformation of prisoners and especially of juvenile offenders. They welcome and largely use the efforts of volunteers from outside, and have no doubt as to the benefit of Sunday schools, and lectures on moral and industrial subjects. But if I were to suggest these as desirable here and now I might find a medical inspector sent to test my sanity." And in my last report, dated January 11, 1886, I wrote, "I should like to put on record a suggestion that the removal of this prison might well be made the occasion of the establishment of a special house of detention,

How Criminals are Made and Prevented

after the nature of a truant school, to which all boys and girls under sixteen might be remanded instead of their being introduced to a prison, and that frequently without having committed any crime. People hardly believe me when I say that I have been called upon to minister to children of both sexes, aged six and seven, confined for a week in separate cells as remanded. This is happily impossible now, owing to the action of the late Home-Secretary (Harcourt); but the time is not far distant when people will find it equally hard to believe that any children in 1885 were sent here simply for being homeless and friendless, and as such committing the 'crime' of sleeping out. Besides the more obvious objections to this state of affairs there is no doubt that the comparative luxury of a prison removes from the street arab nearly all the deterrent force the idea of a prison had before, and his return as a real criminal is rendered more likely. When any School Board can set up its Truant School, with power of detention, the cry of *Non Possumus* on the part of the Home-Office can hardly be raised," and again I pointed to another evil, now happily removed, "that of association in the miserably inadequate accommodation provided at our police-courts. I

Are We Improving ?

can recall many instances of assault and robbery, as well as daily examples of moral harm done in such places." But as I now go through these old reports and earlier writings, on the whole I can testify that hardly a wrong against which I protested now exists, and hardly a reform I desiderated has not come about. It has been with some silent amusement that I have heard the flourish of trumpets which accompanied some improvement, for suggesting which years beforehand I was ignored or even snubbed. These reforms have had their share in causing recent convictions to reach the lowest point within statistical record, proportionally to population, while the daily average prison population in 1911 was 10,646 less than in the previous year!

If I were asked what is the chief cause of a diminution of crime, and what the chief glory and success of the last thirty years, I should answer Child-saving Work, the recognition of the rights and the importance of the child, and the removal of hindrances to the full development of its life in every department of its being. Ponder this significant fact that in Mr. Garrett's comprehensive "Children and the Law," the Table of Statutes cited contain one statute affecting the rights and the wrongs

How Criminals are Made and Prevented

of children dating from Athelstan, one of Philip and Mary, one of Elizabeth, two of Charles II, one of George II, one of George III, one of George IV, one of William IV; but forty of Victoria, and eight of Edward VII, including the extremely comprehensive Children Act, which codifies, supplements, and improves all preceding Acts. Well for children that they have been born in the last generation: well for us that we have had some share in making their pathway sure and pleasant. Our grandfathers were great on the rights of parents: we have had to enforce their obligations, and, if necessary, to destroy their rights when they are made to injure the child. From the unborn babe to the strapping young man being educated and elevated as a juvenile-adult in a Borstal institution, recent legislation has recognized the importance to the State of its rising generation, and has reduced to impotence the old obstructive and destructive enemies of childhood which sheltered their real nature under the names of "parental rights," "liberty of the subject," and "vested interests." So we have seen the children cleared out from the brothel, the prison, and the workhouse; we have seen the discrediting of institutions and barracks for orphan or destitute children in favour of the

Are We Improving?

system of small and scattered Homes; the casts of the school net being so regular and so efficacious that few children, even of nomad parents, escape its meshes; the advancement of the age at which immunity from school can be claimed (though sixteen should be our aim and our next achievement); the establishment, the extension and the improvement of Day-Truant Schools, of Industrial Schools, of Reformatories (the first reformatory was only opened in 1837, and the first industrial school in 1841); of Children's Courts and Probation Officers; the power of adoption and protection from parents given to guardians of the poor; the illegality of uninspected baby-farms and of insurance of infants by foster-parents; the feeding of all necessitous school-children (unfortunately a permissive Act only); of special schools for the blind, the deaf, the crippled, and the mentally defective; a law that no child shall work in a factory on Sundays or at night, and at the most only on alternate days or half-days, and only while attending school regularly; the abolition of street-begging and of street-trading, except under certain exceptions allowed by local by-laws; the exclusion of school-children from public-houses as messengers or visitors; the invention and the acceptability of

How Criminals are Made and Prevented

Boys' Brigades, gymnasia, clubs, and public recreation grounds; and generally all the Acts which followed the efforts of the great Earl of Shaftesbury to limit child-labour until its practical abolition could be insured. Financially prejudiced parents and employers always opposed the child-protection, which is really the State's self-protection. The former maintained, and to a certain extent even now have room to maintain, that they must have the highest wages at once procurable by the child, without any thought of such policy being penny wise and pound foolish; the latter have invariably resisted legislation on the plea that ruin would ensue if the cheapest labour could not be utilized. But, as Miss Dunlop well says in her "English Apprenticeship and Child-labour, "the regular failure of the events to justify the dismal forebodings of the employers has brought their power of foresight into discredit." Trade has a great power of readjusting itself to new conditions. Farmers are not all ruined because they can no longer have infants of seven years working on their fields. And if a particular trade should become extinct because it could only be profit-earning by means of child-labour, the nation will shed no tear over its grave. England has, even on the part of some unconsciously or

Are We Improving?

unavowedly, been turning to the cave of Bethlehem and the cottage of Nazareth for its pattern, and to the infanticide of Herod as its warning.

This subject naturally leads one on to a review of the progress and the improvement of education, especially in the case of those attending elementary schools. It has been a costly matter, and progress has been accompanied by the wails and protests of the selfish and the shortsighted. Said a Swiss once to me, "We grumble like any Englishman at our rates and taxes; but never at what we have to pay for our schools. That is not loss but investment." If Moderates were only moderators of inconsiderate progress, no one, save a few extremists, would object to their position; but I have not noticed any Progressive proposal or measure in the matter of sanitation or education which they did not oppose at first, however they might adopt or even take credit for it afterwards. Everything is now better and brighter for the school-child than in times I can remember. Looking back through many septennia, each a generation from the school point of view, and with the influence of the hundreds of young minds which have flowed into mine during that wonderful septennium between their seventh and their four-

How Criminals are Made and Prevented

teenth year, one generalization which occurs to me is that if a boy had told me once that he really liked going to school I should have thought him a bit of a humbug, whereas if now he told me he really disliked going to school (I am speaking of day boys of course) I should think him more than a bit of a young ass. From the kindergarten to which babes of five come happily to learn by playing, to the opening of the eyes to marvels in the ex-Seventh Standard; in the lofty and spacious halls for the delights of unmechanical drill and the singing of songs most unlike the street yelling of music-hall ditties of the ancient and baser sort; in the organized games of the playground, which have replaced the vacuousness of the occasional rough horse-play of the street; in the object-lessons, the nature-study, and the school museums; in the picture gallery which grows each year with reproductions of masterpieces in line, in visions of colour which illuminate the drabness of the little streets around, or scenes from other lands which remind us that the squalid slum and even the smug suburb is not all the world has to show us in the future, our children are blessed now and filled with the capacity for greater blessedness to come. The "grinder" and the "usher" are types as extinct

Are We Improving?

as Mrs. Gamp in comparison with the trained nurse in the children's hospital, which again is a Victorian invention. Novel opportunities for adding to their knowledge, and for putting to higher or special use the intellectual tools which elementary education has put in their hands, are within the reach of all by Evening Continuation Classes and the comprehensive Polytechnics, so that all can keep up and advance their knowledge if they choose. Little is left to be done, except that there should be some compulsion to use these advantages until at least the age of sixteen is reached; that there should be a correlation between Evening Schools and Polytechnics so that they should supplement and not compete; and (I strongly think) that children who have reached the Sixth Standard should be passed on at once to a Secondary or Higher Grade School instead of remaining, perhaps for some years, in the Seventh or ex-Seventh Standards in the same school, rather marking-time than advancing, especially when there are not enough of them in that elementary school to make a special class and have a special teacher. While it is by no means true that "Eddication's the panacea," as a publican said in a Temperance Conference in which I took part, yet the vast improvement made in our schools,

How Criminals are Made and Prevented

in addition to schooling having been made compulsory and free, has its undoubted share in the general amelioration of speech and ways, and is a real factor in the decrease of crime or of intemperance.

As regards any improvement in the possibility of the labourer and the artisan obtaining comfort in life and more than bare necessities in his home, I have no doubt whatever as to its existence. Granted abstinence from gambling and tippling, the home is better furnished, thrift is more possible and common, and what seemed thirty years ago unattainable luxuries are now enjoyed by most. Any one who has lived in the same sort of districts as I, will remember, to quote but one matter in proof, how few thought of or found the possibility of a country or seaside holiday a generation ago, and how comparatively common is such a refreshment now. The cheapening of many necessities, and some increase in wage, has mainly contributed to this end. Mentally to recall the few cottages in which a bicycle or a piano could be found in comparison with these things being now almost normal where the home is well ordered, will again be evidence of progress. Where the "half-pint" or the "shilling on a horse" has ceased to be the

Are We Improving?

hobby, the collection of interesting objects, the domestic library, the means and the desire for some form of amusement which shall recreate and not merely distract or excite, is found in many a humble home. It is often a wonder how the poor can save; but they do. When I went to St. Peter's, Walworth, I found in that exclusively poor parish a Parochial Penny Bank with a membership of some four hundred. By starting district visitors and getting them to receive money weekly as they visited, I shortly nearly trebled the number, whereas the amount paid out at Christmas in 1894 was £370, in 1895 it was £500, and in 1896 £664, with 1,033 depositors. Later, we averaged 1,000 members, with £600 paid out at the end of the year besides a considerable amount being withdrawn earlier under special circumstances. And a small Slate Club received in my last six years from its members nearly a thousand pounds.

And as to religion? This was a question put to me when leaving London, and was being butchered to make an interviewer's meat. I see that I answered one, "So far as it is associated with attendance at public worship and common prayer, I regret to say that it is on the decline. It is not the fashion to go to church. Yet, simultaneously,

How Criminals are Made and Prevented

there is more respect shown to-day for religion if the subject is mentioned, and blatant irreligion or atheism is less common. In a public meeting a reference to the religious aspect of a matter is received with veneration, and sometimes enthusiasm, and in the selection of candidates for public office the question of morality and religion has always its weight, and to my knowledge has not seldom caused the rejection of a proposed candidate or secured his not being elected at the next poll. There is neglect of religion without antagonism to it, and it is a personal testimony and influence which is wanted, but not found so generally as it should be, when few but the clergy of the Church of England live in the districts round the place of worship they serve. South London, riparian South London I mean, is certainly more dead as regards the outward profession of religion than other parts of the Metropolis, and the diocese of Southwark is the Lazarus diocese, severed by the "great gulf" of the Thames from the workers and the wealth which pour into East London. The three great damnations of our times are the loss of the power of the conviction of sin amongst multitudes; the loss of the sense of duty in comparison with that of pleasure or of profit; and the loss of

Are We Improving?

the desire for worship, when multitudes think they show their religious instincts by ever desiring to hear some new thing or new voice rather than by performing the old religious duties. At the back of this is, of course, the growth of emotionalism and of individualism, as to which much might be said and various illustrations given. Still, an optimist is hopeful of the future as well as thankful for the past.

RETURN TO ➡ **CIRCULATION DEPARTMENT**
202 Main Library

LOAN PERIOD 1 **HOME USE**	2	3
4	5	6

ALL BOOKS MAY BE RECALLED AFTER 7 DAYS
1-month loans may be renewed by calling 642-3405
6-month loans may be recharged by bringing books to Circulation Desk
Renewals and recharges may be made 4 days prior to due date

DUE AS STAMPED BELOW

JUL 12 1992

CIRCULATION DEPT.

UNIVERSITY OF CALIFORNIA, BERKELEY
FORM NO. DD6, 60m, 12/80   BERKELEY CA 94720

280208

UNIVERSITY OF CALIFORNIA LIBRARY

Printed in Great Britain
by Amazon.co.uk, Ltd.,
Marston Gate.